1 —

THE PLATINUM PROJECT

Cynthia Hurst

The Platinum Project

Send written inquiries to:
P.O. Box 6400, Vero Beach, Florida 32961
For electronic inquiries: www.cynthiahurst.com

ISBN: 978-0-9838832-0-3

Printed in the United States of America

FIRST EDITION

This is a work of nonfiction. Any inaccuracies are unintentional. A few names, people and places have been changed to protect individual privacy.

Front cover art: Alchemical symbol for platinum made by joining the symbols of silver and gold. Honeycomb background shows inside pattern of a catalytic converter. Graphic artwork provided by Brian Holmes.
Back cover art: Author photo by Richard Hurst

Published by: WRB Publishing
Palm City, Florida
wrb1174@att.net

For my dad, Robert William Boyce,
And my grandfathers,
Samuel Bernard Boyce and Fred John Krott
In memoriam

Table of Contents

Acknowledgments

Thank you to all the men who bit the bullet and wrote something or agreed to have me write about them. This book runs the gamut, from going fishing to surviving a revolution, and gives a true picture of men in the 21st century, simply because some great guys took the time to reveal a little about themselves and what life is like for them. I am proud to know all of you, and I owe each of you a debt of gratitude.

Thanks also to Joyce Levi for proofreading and offering comments.

Cynthia Callander is an old friend with new ideas for publicity, marketing, and support. She represents the Vero Beach Book Center well, and the entire staff is a continual source of promotion and delight. Thank you again for all your efforts on my behalf. (We are learning together to live with electronic media as we hold on desperately to the look and smell and feel of a real book in our hands!)

Brian Holmes was new to this project (and my life) and offered his brilliant talents with graphic arts and cover design. It was a pleasure to make your acquaintance, and it continues as I get to know you and your family.

Finally, thanks to all the people in the background who lent a hand in even the smallest way to make the big dream of this book become a reality.

Author's note: Opinions expressed are those of the individual writers and do not necessarily reflect the views of the author/editor. Some permissiveness in grammar and writing styles was granted in the interest of creativity. Every effort was made to be factually accurate. Any misinformation or errors that may have slipped through the cracks are mine.

Preface

Platinum is an extremely rare metal, occurring at a concentration of only 0.005 ppm in the Earth's crust. Because of its rarity, King Louis XV of France declared it the only metal fit for a king. On a luxury level, platinum is the precious metal of choice for diamond engagement rings because of its inertness and shine. Unlike gold, another popular choice due to its richness and appearance, platinum does not wear out; unlike silver, it does not tarnish. (The plump fish on the cover is the alchemical symbol for platinum, combining the symbols for silver and gold.) Rolex uses platinum for their limited edition watch series. Platinum credit cards are better than gold ones. An album that sells a million copies is said to have "gone platinum." On a practical level, applications span from cancer drugs to catalytic converters.

My point here is that *platinum* is a term of distinction, whether it be jewelry, the metal industry, the stock market, or recording history. It is an achievement that indicates quality, strength, savvy; a standard of measurement for success that is universally understood. Platinum has substance, and it endures.

The Platinum Project: MEN in the 21st Century describes men of the same caliber. Together these articles, essays, and literary pieces portray a picture of adventure and steadfastness, humor and irony, variety and virility, philosophical and scientific pursuits, of men in the 21st century. It is a companion piece to *The Diamond Project: Ordinary Women Leading Extraordinary Lives*, albeit a little edgier and grittier, as a manly book should be.

In prehistoric times, all platinum was buried beneath the earth and all men were hunters. In the millennium age, platinum is mined in Columbia and the Ural mountains of Russia and the Sudbury Basin in Canada, and has a number of industrial, practical, and modern uses. By the same token, men (ahem, most) are no longer cavemen, and few make their living hunting. The diversity and possibility and opportunity for discovery open to them are limitless.

There is a hunger out there on the part of men: for reassurance that they are headed in the right direction and getting some things accomplished; affirmation through daring-do activities and sports that test their boundaries and abilities; and confirmation that they can find meaning—and yes, happiness—in a competitive, technological world. Men want to know their lives make a difference. They pursue dreams. They laugh at themselves. (And seem to possess the uniquely male distinction of finding the *Honeymooners,* the *Three Stooges,* and *Monty Python* hilariously funny.) But they still go to battle for what they believe in and still believe love makes the world go 'round.

Most mornings I walk to the beach to see what sand and sea and sky are doing that day. It's almost always sunny, but recently when I took the few steps up to the gazebo leading to the boardwalk and down to the beach, the ocean was not there. It had disappeared, hidden by a gray shroud of fog. The sun was trying to poke its way through the haze and by 10 a.m. was victorious. The day moved toward flawless.

The men who contributed their stories for this book are like that. Doubt and obscurity may drift in at night on occasion, dispelled by new courage and resolve in the light of day. I was amazed by what I uncovered—not hidden secrets exactly—but fascinating aspects of every man, as yet undisclosed because no one had ever asked.

Like platinum, they begin rough and imbedded in other substances, but are refined as they grow older and continually seek the tools of improvement. They have all shown their mettle *(metal?)*. Between Superman-steel and Clark Kent-aluminum lies a vast network of potential and skill. None of them are perfect. None of them are boring. Perfect is boring.

So sit back and brace yourselves for some dangerous escapades, fierce loyalties, executives and musicians, soldiers and survivors, spiritual revelations and earthbound truths, an inventor and even a couple of hunters, from men I have encountered all over the world and have come to know better — and become quite fond of — through these pages. For to quote Han Solo, *Here's where the fun begins.*

Story of the Abbotts

David D. Abbott

David Abbott lives with his wife, Jane, in a rambling but well-kept home located in the beautiful area of Cardinal, Virginia, near the town of Marshall, on a waterway near the Chesapeake Bay. Jane's father was a crab fisherman, and she grew up with boats and water living. David, too, shares a love of the water and the wildlife around them. Shade oaks and maples surround the place. The loft of their barn has been converted into a modern office and computer room. Both David and Jane are Master Gardeners and reserve part of their acreage to plant herbs, flowers, and a vegetable garden. David is also a collector, and their home contains all kinds of interesting, possibly worthless, (or not?) objects. The Abbotts are the parents of two sons, John and Daniel. Daniel died as a young man. John married the lovely Ana and together they produced a grandson, named for his brother. They live in Arizona. David did not write about any of this. He writes about the past. But it leads him to who he is today – a man able to adapt to change and learn from his family history – alive and well in the 21st century.

In the Christian year of 1641, George Abbot, a Unitarian minister, sailed from England for Boston. By 1643, he had settled in Andover and built his house as a fort to resist the earlier Americans. Our great (to the 10th power) grandfather survived and prospered. Abbott, as a name, is a thread that runs through the entire fabric of American history. There were Abbots and Abbotts. There were Abbotts among the Pilgrim Fathers, Abbotts among the first settlers of the colonies, Abbotts who fought their way on the old frontiers, and Abbotts who later hewed through wilderness and traversed deserts and mountains to settle on the new frontiers.

One early Abbott, Daniel, born in Massachusetts, was taken by an Indian tribe as a slave. After some time, a war party came back with booty from another raid. Part of what they had stolen included ice skates. As they tried to use them, they slipped and fell here and there on the river. Daniel laughed. As punishment, the Indians made him put on the skates and pushed him out onto the ice. Daniel slipped and fell, all the way to the center of the river, as the Indians laughed at him. He then stood up, waved goodbye and skated away, down the river to home.

About two hundred years later, Webster H. Abbott, then native of Michigan, began to explore his future. He and all his brothers of age served in the Civil War with the Union Army. Fortunately he kept a diary which has survived. Webster was first sent to Virginia near Washington, then west toward Bull Run as part of the reserves, then back to the Washington area for most of the winter. In March, they were transported to Fort Monroe in Virginia by steamship. From the diary, it is discovered that one of the things he enjoyed was eating oysters right off the beaches. He was part of the force that marched from the fort to Big Bethel Church to find that the rebels had already deserted it. But they continued, eventually to Yorktown and Williamsburg.

As many in those years, he was frequently sick, and finally he contracted an illness which resulted in disability and discharge from the Army. Perhaps it was the raw oysters in a land where there was no sanitary system. Anyway, he survived, was honorably discharged, and returned to Michigan.

In 1867, Webster Abbott went west and traveled through Kansas to Texas. At Kansas City, he had purchased a stock of cheap watches and jewelry for trading and had thought to engage in a bartering business with the Indians. His wagon train had passed thru the section of Colorado where Trinidad now is. That was in 1867 or 1868, his journey at that time taking him as far south as Silver City, New Mexico. Later he had removed to Comanche County, Texas, where he set up on a farm with sheep.

Here Webster Abbott met, wooed and won the daughter of a rebel soldier. Of this union, two sons and three daughters were born. Their first child, Henry Eugene, was born in their adobe cabin in 1878. Due to a change in economics, ranching became a bad business, and so, great-great-Grandfather moved his family to Dublin, Texas, where he set up in a general merchandise store, and traded in hides and pelts. Here also Henry went to school. A disastrous fire swept the small Texas town and burned out Webster's store, which led to the decision to move to Trinidad, Colorado. This was a very good move for Henry Eugene, who was then about nine years old. His early schooling in Trinidad was at a public school and he later graduated from the privately owned Tillotson Academy in 1896. The next year, while his father had purchased a machine shop, Henry and an older man opened a repair shop.

In December 1900, Henry left his repair shop and enlisted in the U.S. Army, giving his occupation as "carpenter," and requested to be sent to the Philippines. Since he spoke fluent Spanish, he served as interpreter and translator for General Jacob "Howling Jack" Smith on the island of Samar. This was the general whose name became notorious for the "terrible treatment" of the Filipinos by the *water cure*.* After the end of the war there, Henry was discharged from the Army and took the position of Customs Inspector on the island of Cebu. In 1904, he returned to Trinidad and in 1905 he married. Their first child was born in 1906 and named Henry Eugene Abbott Jr.

Henry Sr. worked for others at the Trinidad Novelty Works for a time and then set up his own Abbott Novelty Works. He became the town locksmith, gunsmith, and general repairs mechanic. Where he had learned those skills is unknown but he did very well. He conducted this business until 1917, when the entry of the United States into the World War brought him again into the uniform of Uncle Sam. And the world was opened as a new book of experiences for Henry Abbott.

In 1917, Abbott entered the Second Reserve Officers Training Camp at Fort Sheridan, Illinois. He became first lieutenant of infantry, being transferred as first lieutenant of the aviation section of the signal corps, which is now known as the air service. Abbott was in the engineering unit or division, whatever is the proper military reference. He was now serving in his second war.

Lt. Abbott became an officer of responsible duties. He was sent to Princeton University and to the Massachusetts Institute of Technology at Boston for postgraduate work. Then he was ordered to Fort Worth, Texas, for service with the engineering corps at the Canadian flying field (Taliaferro Field). Here Abbott learned to fly the government planes. Later he was sent to New York as an engineer officer on the Handley-Page bombing squadron, equipped for overseas service, but Abbott never got overseas. The Armistice on November 18, 1918, caught him in New York getting ready to cross the water.

After the Armistice, Lt. Abbott remained in the service. On January 1, 1919, he was made disbursing officer at Hazleton Field, Long Island, and remained there until his honorable discharge, when he returned to Trinidad and re-opened the Abbott Novelty Works.

An outstanding task was laid before him. The town bank caught fire and burned down. The steel safe survived the fire, but when the bankers tried to open the safe, the combination dial would not turn. Using brute force and ignorance, they managed to twist the dial right off the door. *Then* they went to Mr. Abbott. Abbott aligned the dial and re-attached it to the door. He then had kindling and firewood stacked around the safe and lit the fire. When the safe was hot enough, the dial could be turned and he ran the combination to unlock the door bolts. He then turned the bolt handle but did NOT open the door. The fire was then put out and guards protected the safe overnight. The next morning, the safe was cool and he swung the door open for the bankers. The contents had been singed a bit but nothing was lost.

Meanwhile, Henry Junior had been growing and developing the personal skills which led him on to a full life. After graduating from high school, he went on to a degree in geology from the University of Colorado. Unfortunately, his graduation coincided with the beginning of the Depression and there were no jobs to be found in geology. So, what did he do?

Since he was an officer in the Army Air Force (Reserve), he commanded a CCC camp for a number of years. Then he took a job as school teacher. From there, he was elected Superintendent of Schools for his county. During part of this time, he guided the unemployed men near his school to process the "scrap" ore from a gold mine to recover any missed gold. There was enough gold extracted to keep the families fed. And he married another teacher, Alberta, who was the daughter of a teacher.

His father, Henry Sr., died in October 1940. Seven months later, before WW II began (for us), the Abbotts had their first and only child—a boy they named David (this would be me).

Lt. Henry Abbott Jr. was put on active duty and was assigned to Trinidad. Of course, it was not Trinidad, Colorado, but Trinidad, British West Indies. The United States had an airfield on Trinidad that was to be used as one of the rest and refueling stops in ferrying combat planes to Africa. Henry was second in command for about two years and then was promoted to Captain. At that point, his assignment was changed. He was put in charge of building and operating a second airfield on the other side of the Island in order to improve access for increasing traffic.

During the war, David had the very good fortune to have two teachers, his mother and grandmother, raise him for his first four years. That was a real running start!

Finally the war was over, but instead of coming home, Henry was sent directly to a new assignment in Sacramento where his family met him. A year later, he was sent to New York to study at Columbia University. From there, another and another and another, etc., change of assignment followed about every three years. Most were secret and he could not discuss them. His next-to-last assignment was back to New York, where he had the opportunity to return to Columbia and add a doctorate to his two master's degrees. Then there was one more year in the Air Force, this time in San Antonio.

Finally, he retired, moved back to Virginia and went to work—at least, that is what he said. He held several positions with Department of Defense contractors leading to vice president of a small human engineering company. His most important, non-classified, human engineering project there was design layout for the pilot's instruments and controls of the Apollo Lunar Lander.

With all those moves from place to place and school to school, David had learned how to fit in with new friends and to not miss the previous friends, as most were out of his life forever. He had also learned self-reliance and responsibility. At the age of nine, he got a job delivering newspapers in his neighborhood. That lasted two years, until yet another family move took them from Virginia to Maryland. In Virginia, David had started making and building "things" in the basement shop. The basement in Maryland was larger and better lighted and the work bench bigger. More things could be made. Most things were made of wood, but one steel knife was hand-forged from an old discarded file.

As he came of an age, firearms entered his life. He was given a .22 for Christmas and was allowed to store the other family long guns in a closet in his room. At first, the .22 was used for safety and target training; then some of the more powerful guns were used. In the meantime, all the guns were kept clean and dry and never misused.

Speaking of misusing, like many boys David was interested in making small rockets. One of them blew up right in front of him. Fortunately he was wearing glasses, which saved his eyes from the black powder thrown into his face. Though painful, it was an excellent lesson that was never repeated.

Then there were two more moves and graduation from high school in San Antonio. Off to college at Virginia Tech, David entered the Mechanical Engineering curriculum but changed to Engineering Mechanics in his second school quarter. (Engineering Mechanics is a much broader dip into engineering than M.E.; it seems mostly like applied physics during the undergraduate years.) He also joined the Co-op program so he could earn money and get practical experience at the same time. Co-op students work alternate quarters of each year and attend school the other quarters. His first five quarters of Co-op working were at the Dahlgren Naval Weapons Laboratory.

The first two quarters were in an engineering office, making drawings for and calculations about the mass properties of an anti-radar missile warhead. That was particularly good as an introduction to engineering calculations, but the missile project was canceled and David moved from the engineering office to the explosives research office. Oh boy! Here he got hands-on (literally) experience with high explosives and dynamic testing procedures.

His final two quarters of Co-op work were with a small defense contractor that was developing new firearms and ammunitions for the Army. He excelled at this work and introduced improvements to the firearms.

During his school quarters, David had the good fortune to meet his future wife, Jane, when both took a summer class in Engineering Calculus.

After graduation, David took a full-time job with the defense contractor. That lasted seven years and he was awarded a number of patents for ammunitions and their manufacturing methods. He also applied some of the explosives education from the Dahlgren job for a DOD project (classified).

He left that company and took a short-term job with a company that developed plastic extrusion processes and equipment. Two inventions, not patented, but held in-house, were developed there. After some time, David sought a change and worked for a multi-branched, private manufacturing company. There he worked on several different projects that also required inventions which were not patented but kept as company secrets.

The next position was with the Qyx division of Exxon. Qyx was the name of a very advanced typewriter, driven by stepper motors which were controlled by electronic sensors and special programmable circuits. This development began in the very early days of personal computers. It pre-dated desktop printers. The printing was by delivery of impact energy to text characters mounted on a rotating wheel of such characters. After several years of development and early manufacturing, Exxon management decided to close the Qyx division and drop the people down the "drill hole."

One final full-time job in electronics/printing went down a similar hole when that company was subjected to a leveraged buy-out.

Eventually, David decided that he could manage his life better as a consultant than as an employee. The first customer was another DOD contractor who was developing military ammunition. That was a bit of fun and resulted in another in-house invention.

David really enjoyed the next contract. A pharmaceutical company had contracted with an electronics company to solve a number of problems with a European device which turned liquid medicine into a breathable fog for treatment of breathing difficulties. The electronics company needed an engineer who could apply physics and logic to electro-mechanical devices. David was called in by the owner of the electronics company who knew him from previous work. The long and short of it is that another invention solved the biggest problem and this one was patented. It solved the major problem and all else was easy.

David has now stopped consulting since it gets in the way of fishing and other important things, but he still has a few inventions to develop for himself.

He and Jane have visited Andover and seen the several hundred graves of the Abbotts there. A large granite monument was placed in the graveyard of East Church commemorating George Abbot.   The inscription on the stone is detailed, describing him as born in England and "one of the first settlers of Andover, A.D. 1643" — which returns us to the opening lines of this missive.

*Editor's note: The water cure employed by General Smith was the same method we have come to know as waterboarding: a man is thrown on his back, held down, and water forced onto his face, down his throat and nose until he "gives" or is rendered unconscious. The suffering is compared to one who is drowning but not allowed to drown. Waterboarding was deemed to be a crime by the Republican president of the United States at the time: Theodore Roosevelt. He ordered the court martial of General "Howling Jack" Smith, who got his name when he directed troops to reduce a particular province to a "howling wilderness." When Smith was cleared of war crimes charges, Roosevelt insisted on "the right to review" and had him thrown out of the army. – Philadelphia Inquirer 05/01/2009

Cruising on Southbend

Walter Russell Bodie

Walter R. Bodie started his own publishing business when he retired from his work with Miami-Dade forensics and wanted to make things easier for his wife, Leona, a Florida Treasure Coast writer. She suggested I get a competitive quote from him when I wrote the companion piece to this book, **The Diamond Project.** *I found Walt easy to work with, reasonably priced, professional in all endeavors, and just plain interesting. His wife is Portuguese and, together with his German stock, they make beautiful things (and offspring) together. Of course, I was very interested in his CSI (Crime Scene Investigation) background, since his field is the subject of several TV shows and spin-offs and a hot topic of the times. But I never expected to receive this fascinating and dramatic account in return. You might want to consider wearing a helmet for this one.*

Southbend Boulevard was a clear shot. My body was drenched in sunset hues. If only I could slow the day, quickening into night. For all my wishful thinking, the crimson clouds faded into grays and darkened. How could such a moment be ominous? I didn't know it, but at that moment I was on a two-lane road to hell.

I considered myself a cautious driver who always drove defensively. Hey, when you have a life as good as this one, you protect it. That reminded me of my last annual physical when my doctor commented, "Walter, you have the body of a thirty-year-old."

"Great." I certainly didn't see myself as a typical senior citizen, and bragged, "My weight's exactly the same as it was in high school."

Youth recaptured at seventy. Yep, that's the freedom and power I felt every time I rode my motor scooter. Here I was on the open road, riding in my zone. Nope, I'd never be an old fogey. I savored the rush at 40 mph, as the breezes whipped past my tanned cheeks and swept my streaked hair across my forehead. So free. Pure fun, no worries. No TV, phones, computers. No task other than watching the road.

I gloried in the view and reminded myself how carefree I felt earlier that afternoon, cruising on Indian River Lagoon aboard my skiff, *Relaxation Station.* An unexpected spray refreshed me as the sun basted my back. I headed for a nearby barrier island, listening to Jimmy Buffet tunes with my youngest son. Unlike his older brother, James (the sales pro), my younger son, at age thirty-one, was an Orange County firefighter/paramedic/engineer with a master's degree in international business. Wayne loved boating, swimming, snorkeling and scuba diving—almost a clone, we had so much in common. In some ways more fish than mammal, I smiled. But I soon dismissed the insight and concentrated on the road.

For me, life's meant to be lived with passion and to the hilt, and no jousting was about to cut me down prematurely. Like my motorcycle before it, my scooter delivered liberty, speed and adventure. Such a thrill—and I'd filled my tank for less than three dollars. My 2008 Chinese, 150cc Qlink Pegasus cruised at a speed where one road stripe after another forged an unbroken white line. Above the drone of the engine, the wind gushed in a high-pitched whistle.

Almost there, to the cottage on Hidden River where my wife, Leona, waited. She called it pretty—and it was—but I preferred the dock and gazebo. It was close now. This particular Wednesday, I felt high on life after traveling a hundred miles on the scooter. Although I was happily married, I appreciated my alone times. This was one of those times. Other than boating (and I had owned five boats, from sailboats to trawlers), nothing else relaxed me as much as riding a motorcycle. That symbiosis of rider and machine was unique. Cruising on Southbend delivered the great escape, like a theme park featuring unlimited rides and great shows.

Only four more miles to go. Not another vehicle on the road. I *owned* this stretch of public real estate by the Jessica McClintock Park, a breadth of green palms under a splotchy sky. Almost there; only a hundred feet from the curve...

Oh God! Holy shit! That bastard can't pull out in front of me. Can't the crazy fool see my headlights? The pickup truck *had* to stop in time. It screeched. The Pegasus skidded. My brakes locked. An instant stretched in slow motion as acrid fumes of rubber fused into asphalt and burned my nostrils before I catapulted. Airborne. Lifted higher. Weightless. Then nothingness.

"Walter, wake up," her voice crooned.

"Mom, what are you doing here?"

"*Mein Sohn*," she said with a strong German accent, "you know I love you."

"It's been so long."

"Walter, why weren't you wearing a helmet? Even an immigrant knows these things."

"There's no law that says I have to."

"Have you seen your face? So much blood; so much road rash. Your mouth is swollen, *Liebling*, your teeth, your beautiful teeth. Your jaw is broken."

"But, Mom, you're dead. I ..."

"Perhaps. Close your eyes now and rest. Leona will be here soon."

The image in my head the next time I opened my eyes was not of my wife. Rather, I awoke in time for my blue-letter day — a bachelor's degree in chemistry — the first Bodie in my family's history to graduate from college. Class of 1962. As I scanned the flotilla of heads in the Penn State University auditorium, the vision of a slight, five-foot-two-inch frame crystallized. My mother sat perfectly straight, like all my German relatives, wearing her brightest smile below her pillbox hat. Her gloved hand held a hankie and she gently dabbed at joyful tears.

I wanted to see her there and, even more so, both my parents together. They'd divorced when I was ten. Instead, I saw my dad smiling at me, pride and love written all over his face, my stepmother seated beside him. I tucked my disappointment into a private hidden place, then cradled my diploma and sighed as my mother's vision slipped away. At that moment I pondered the irony of my mother and stepmother sharing the same name: Mildred.

Riding my motorcycle cleared my mind, allowed me to think with utter clarity.

A year zipped by faster than the new high-speed rail in China. And that's where I landed after my first job with Goodyear Tire & Rubber. Fortunately, it passed high-speed in retrospect, because the reality of that one-year job was more like a slow boat to China. I envisioned the promotion I had done for them, driving a tractor across America. Damn, Maine was cold, even in July! Next thing I knew, I had joined the Navy and was assigned to a destroyer as a machinist mate. For a while, serving in the military meant nothing more complicated than following orders, a few bar fights, and sexual escapades in every port.

That is, until President Johnson escalated the war, commencing air strikes on North Vietnam and committing ground forces. My destroyer was deployed from Norfolk, Virginia, to Subic Bay in the Philippine Islands where we re-provisioned. From there, my ship operated in the waters off Vietnam. My commanding officer briefed us. "The Vietnam Navy consists of high-speed torpedo boats," he told us. "Destroy them!" Since their boats moved faster than our ship's fire-control radar could track, several sister ships were lost. The mission failed.

That crushing blow led me and my comrades to try other tactics. Something viable finally emerged. After firing Flak, normally used for anti-aircraft gunfire, super-hot projectiles rained onto the enemy's wooden boats, setting them afire before they could launch their torpedoes. We made short work of the Vietnamese Navy until the Chinese sent metal boats through the Tonkin Gulf. To defeat this new threat, we maneuvered to the border between China and Vietnam, where one night we spotted a fleet of Chinese boats and radioed the carrier to send its combat jets. Come dawn, after the U.S. jets decimated the entire Vietnam Navy, I stood topside and watched hundreds of venomous sea snakes crawling on the water's surface. After several minutes, I slipped below deck, fell on my bunk, and dreamed of more pleasant things, like home.

My tours of the Panama Canal, Hawaii, the Philippines, India, Hong Kong, China, and Taiwan transformed me. But the Vietnam War affected me even more. Although I'd survived the horrors of war, I never forgot those who were not so fortunate.

Like most soldiers, too young for the job. Some exposed to blood, pain, and gore. Others to Agent Orange. Many cheated of their futures, robbed of their lives. They all wanted to be home like I was. My eyes watered and I couldn't keep them open. Mom asked, "Are your allergies kicking up again?"

Grateful and aware of how fortunate I was to be back in New Jersey, with my life and all my body parts intact, I had a new life as a chemist for Campbell Soup. Eight years passed before I met Leona. I saw her at the Waterwheel, a *Cheers* vibe, and stood transfixed. Those seconds stretched into eons. Enough time to memorize her face, smile, and signature laugh. Together they etched a pattern on my heart. Three months later on Rehoboth Beach, I asked her to marry me. Our wedding day, November 27, turned out to be an unseasonably warm, spectacular day.

At least we suffered through that first New Jersey winter together. However, young love didn't compensate for the challenges of a particularly harsh Atlantic Coast winter with record lows. After carving both cars out of an icy parking lot three times in one week, I convinced Leona that Florida living was for us. Before I caught my breath as a chemist for Airco, I morphed into a quality assurance specialist for a Miami medical device company.

My personal profile was evolving, too. Now that I was the father of two sons, it seemed terribly important to instill in them my own passions and values. Those years blurred, and in a microsecond I was taking my oldest son James to the University of Ohio.

Professionally, my enthusiasm for my new job soured as the years zoomed by. I was stressed out. I also suspected the executive staff of criminal wrongdoing. But before I could blow the whistle, I was hired by the Dade County Police Department.

Unbeknownst to me, Leona had mailed them my resume, and apparently they liked what they saw. They held my resume for six months and then called me for an interview. I was offered, and accepted, a position as a forensic specialist and expert witness for the department. I worked in the MDPD crime lab for twenty-one years.

Crime knew no boundaries, and victims ranged from children like Adam Walsh to adult drug trafficking. At the Miami-Dade crime lab, several of my cases made national headlines. One such case, The Tamiami Strangler, involved the murders of prostitutes along the Tamiami Trail in Little Havana. Six desperate souls who sold their bodies for one more high. The perpetrator raped and strangled his victims, then moved their bodies to other neighborhoods, leaving teaser notes. He wrote on one victim's back with black magic marker, *See If You Can Catch Me*.

My work mattered. I was saving lives. The analysis and testimony I provided helped put this killer behind bars and on Death Row. I understood Miami's underbelly and the critical role forensics played in solving crimes. Those twenty-one years felt like a lifetime between two heartbeats when I retired.

Retirement. That's why I now had time to enjoy cruising in the Bahamas, reveling in the unspoiled beaches and surreal sunsets of the Out Islands. Four years later, I was a graphic artist with my own publishing company, helping my wife and other writers achieve their dreams. Imagine me subcontracting to other publishers. Imagine me affiliated with the most comprehensive bookselling channel in the industry in the United States and the United Kingdom, including distribution partners Ingram, Baker & Taylor, Amazon.com, and Barnes & Noble. Imagine giving military veterans and aspiring and established writers a channel to voice their stories. Part-time though, leaving me with plenty of adventures ahead.

What's that noise? I wondered as the chopping sounds of a trauma helicopter intruded on my musings. I didn't grasp that in real time I was starring in a fast-paced suspense drama full of twists and turns—engaged in a battle and suffering through my own brush with death. Fire Rescue arrived seven minutes later to pry me from the pickup truck's undercarriage, where I lay wedged between the tires. I felt nothing. When I awoke in the trauma center hours later, I didn't know my name. Every part of my body hurt, except the severed top jaw that rested on my tongue. My wife's warm hand squeezed my cold, limp one—that I knew.

A day later, my teeth and jaw were anchored into place with surgical wire. After eight weeks of liquids, I underwent four root canals in three hours, and contemplated the Guinness world record of six in a day. *Damn, at some point a hamburger's gonna taste good!*

At home and seemingly on the mend, I blacked out for several seconds, falling like a dead weight onto the tile floor. When I awoke with a piercing pain from a fractured rib, my son James put a pillow under my head and tended to me until the paramedics took over. At the ER, the doctor explained, "Too much trauma."

Already March 19 and two months after the accident, I only felt 80 percent. Where was that body of a thirty-year-old? I felt a hundred. With more healing expected in the upcoming months, my doctors and surgeons told me, "Last month one of our physicians died in a motorcycle accident. *Don't you ever ride again without a helmet! And if you're still wondering what to do about your scooter, sell it!* You're an incredibly lucky guy with plenty of adventures ahead." By April 19, I believed him. I felt 99 percent.

At long last, the two-lane road to hell drifted away, leaving a beautiful Florida sunset over Hidden River. Leona and I sat in the gazebo, took it all in, and quietly held hands.

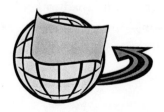

Man of the World Made in Detroit

Daniel J. Boyce

Daniel Joseph Boyce is my baby brother. Of the twelve of us, I was born first, followed by four brothers, then four sisters, then Danny, and then two more sisters to complete the Boyce family dozen. Dan has been a numbers guy – and a Detroit team sports fan--since he was a kid. He always kept these spiral notebooks loaded with numbers, statistics, sports picks and scores. It is not surprising that he grew up to be an accountant. And with his lasting faith in a city like Detroit that has failed so many times for so many people, it is not surprising that he started a club called "Detroiters at Heart." Today he is an executive for the World Bank based in Washington, D.C., assigned to places like Mexico, Central and South America, Nepal and Sri Lanka. He e-mails photos of himself from the Maldives, standing in the midst of a group of children from the village, all smiles. His current job title is Lead Financial Management Specialist for Latin America and the Caribbean, so add several islands, too. His wife, Veronica, from Ecuador, also works with the World Bank. Possessing two left feet, Dan took salsa lessons for their wedding just to impress his bride, who dances as if she were born to it. The busiest people are always the ones who do the most, and I couldn't be prouder of my brother, or happier that he not only agreed to write, but made good on his promise. Dan wrote this while on a plane to Columbia. Or was it Costa Rica?

Possible angles:
Option 1: How does a kid from Detroit end up as a Spanish-speaking, international accountant at the World Bank?
Option 2: Opportunity and the road less traveled.
Option 3: White and black and Latino all over (*Mi Mundo en Blanco y Negro*).

My journey to an international life has been largely via "roads less traveled by." When faced with choices about what university to attend, what to study, or where to work, I have followed my heart as well as my mind, while those around me often followed the herd.

The first major fork in the road appeared before me on a normal day at Benedictine High School in 1983. Sister Pat, our friendly but usually uninspiring guidance counselor, stopped me in the hallway between classes. "Dan, can you go to a meeting?" she asked. "There is this university here from Florida. They make a big effort to recruit in Detroit but we need more people at their presentation."

More reluctant than excited, I went to the recruiting session. It was not the usual pitch. There was Dr. Norman Johnson, Assistant Dean of the School of Business and Industry at Florida A&M University, who, like any good salesman, seemed to have all the angles covered. Dr. Johnson handed out a package of materials that included articles from *Newsweek* and *Fortune* magazine with titles like "Watch out Harvard, here's Florida A&M." He talked of scholarships based on straightforward criteria. Internships with big companies around the country. Good jobs. I had never seen anything like this from the Michigan schools that passed through Benedictine. As I sifted through the materials, full of young, sharp-looking African American kids in business attire, one obvious question came to mind. So when the time came I put my hand straight up and asked Dr. Johnson, "Are these opportunities available to *white* students?"

Well yes, they were. And for this white kid growing up in mostly black northwest Detroit, seeing that opportunity and taking it was the first in a series of fortunate decisions in my life.

My mother and father made two trips out of Michigan during my time at Florida A&M: one to drop me off in 1984, and one to pick me up in 1988. Both trips were by car, twenty hours down I-75. In fact, my father died in 1990, somewhat proudly having never been on an airplane. At my business school graduation, a parent of each of the fifty graduates — including the lone white one — was expected to say a few words. As I listened to my classmates, it seemed like all of them were introducing their father and mentioning his business pursuits. I got the best laugh of the day by starting with "My father is definitely *not* a black businessman."

The adventure of attending a historically black university was followed by two years in a normal job as an auditor at one of the big accounting firms in Chicago. Long before those two years were up, my heart was saying: *I have to do something international.* I went to the library, researched graduate programs, and was determined to find one that would give me the freedom to study subjects I was not able to fit into my accounting curriculum. Before I knew it, still without a passport, I was in a PhD program in Political Science at UCLA, where my best-laid plan was to study French and work in Africa. I even bought audio tapes of the Hausa language and practiced making its unusual sounds over the summer, before flying from Detroit to Los Angeles for my first year of the Master's/PhD program.

My best friend at UCLA was a sophisticated Lebanese woman, Florence Eid, who already seemed to be more international than I could ever dream of becoming. Within a few months of being on campus, Florence questioned the value of French — not to mention Hausa — for an American looking to have an international career. "Spanish is spoken by four million people in Los Angeles alone" was her nice way of saying *what in the hell are you doing studying Hausa?* Hearing this advice — along with a presentation by a student who talked of being "sick every day for a year while I was in Africa" — was enough for me to change course and jump into my first Spanish class at twenty-four years old. It was in that class that I wrote an essay about sitting in a café in Buenos Aires, one of my many dreams at the time and one I was not fully confident would ever be realized.

Three years into my studies at UCLA, with new passport finally in hand and first trip out of North America (to Costa Rica) under my belt, I again credit Florence for placing an opportunity in front of me that changed my life. She showed me a summer internship application for the World Bank, an agency she longed to work for but one of which meant nothing to me. As with the Florida A&M recruiting session, I distinctly remember having a reluctance to fill out the summer internship application, but with Florence's encouragement ("It is only two pages, Dan, why not try?"), I went ahead and mailed it in before the deadline.

At the same time I applied for the World Bank internship, I got connected to Jim Wesberry, a legendary figure in international financial management. Jim was living in New York, and heading a team that was bidding for a contract to establish a new accounting program at a university in Bolivia, and (I think mainly out of the kindness of his heart) he added me to his team. Having no idea what I might be getting into, I bugged Mr. Wesberry's office every few days to see if indeed I was going to be spending my next nine months in Bolivia. After weeks of calling to see if our team had won the contract, one day Jim's office told me "Mr. Wesberry no longer works here. He has gone to work for the World Bank."

With this twist of fate, doors opened from that two-page internship application, and I spent the summer of 1994 in Washington as a Summer Associate with the World Bank. Accepting only two hundred of three thousand prospective summer interns, I felt incredibly lucky to receive one of those spots, and was only grateful my application had fallen into the hands of Jim Wesberry. I was hired into a newly created unit that sought to make World Bank clients more accountable for the funds they borrowed from the Bank. For the first time, a resume of Accounting, Political Science, and Spanish was making sense. Although the internship spanned less than three months, it allowed my *internationalization* to take off at a geometric pace. I started to meet people from all over the world, and see what it was like to work in an international environment.

On one of the last days of the internship, I made a presentation in a training session on how an accounting software package could be used for tracking money in development projects. One of the participants asked if I would like to join him in Peru on his next trip. This would turn out to be the first of dozens of foreign business trips I have taken over the past seventeen years, which included five years living in Mexico.

Just a few years removed from my days as a full-time accountant, I remember thinking that so many basic things about how the world worked had become clearer to me. I had quickly learned so much about who the world's people were and how they lived. I was seeing and hearing things that blew my mind. My roommate at UCLA was a blond-haired, blue-eyed American who spoke fluent Iraqi Arabic, married a Chinese woman, and had political beliefs along the lines of Rush Limbaugh. A PhD student in Persian (aka Iranian) literature, he would spend his free time at the UCLA coffee shop where the "cute Persian chicks" hung out. I would soon learn that most of these extremely attractive young ladies were Jewish—*Jewish Iranians?* This was but one of many revelations of this time in my life. (Wait now, most people from Turkey and Iran are not *Arabs?* Most of the world is not Christian? Costa Rica has no military — none?! And the list goes on....)

By 1998, I was working full-time in Washington at the World Bank, which I realized by then was the largest and most important economic development institution on the planet. At one point in the late 1990s, I calculated that I had left the USA in thirty-six out of thirty-nine months. My work took me to Argentina, Peru, Chile, and many small Caribbean countries. It was exhilarating, but all of the travel definitely had its drawbacks. I wrote the following while on a business trip in 1998:

"I am as happy as can be," I thought.

And then the loneliness set in. This was the other side of the freedom that I was usually pleased to have when traveling alone. The Caribbean islands were especially effective at making you feel cut off – that is in fact their charm for many people. It was not only the fact of being far away from home, with water all around, but there were so many practical barriers — like some of the highest long-distance rates in the world and only limited access to the Internet. The day before, in fact, the telephone lines had been down for a number of hours, making even a phone call to the local Domino's Pizza an impossibility.

Happy … isolated … and sometimes, well, just wanting a slice of pizza.   Yes, a life of shuffling between home and everywhere from Colombia to the Maldives is not all good, but I certainly do not regret taking the paths I have taken.   My Ecuadorian wife, Veronica, and I always have something interesting waiting for us around the corner. We have spent exactly half of our ten years of marriage living in Mexico, the other half in Washington, and visited countless countries and places along the way. While we sometimes wish we could communicate more precisely in each other's languages, or that my job would not separate us so much, we recognize that these issues are small in comparison to the richness that we have when we are together, with friends, or with our parents and siblings in Quito or Motown. (Not to mention Buenos Aires, where I finally made it to that café in March 2011.)

Although I have learned the value of being more strategic in mapping out one's future, I still credit most of my career success to being prepared and open to pounce on opportunities as they come. In fact, I would go so far as to say that I have usually not actively *sought* opportunities—in most cases, they have come to me. Have I had some good luck along the way? Definitely. But far more important has been my ability to seize this good fortune. I have seen similar opportunities presented to many loved ones and colleagues who have allowed them to pass on by. After being unable or unwilling to open door numbers 1, 2, and sometimes 3, they have had to settle for the consolation prize.

What does it mean to be prepared for an opportunity? It starts with the basics: work hard, study hard, and keep your nose (and other body parts) clean.[1] But in addition to these basics, being prepared is also aided by having a vision of what one would like to become.

My own career vision takes me back again to my junior year of high school. As class president, I was locked onto the idea of some day being in politics. As time went on, I set an unofficial target of being the President of the United States, and allowed it to drive my life preparedness program. After all, who needs to be more prepared than our President? While the political dream slowly faded, the idea of building a "presidential resume" served me for many years. I started thinking about what other constituencies and skills I might need beyond those I already had. Grew up in a union family? OK, better study business. White kid in an African-American setting? Learn Spanish. Studied accounting as an undergraduate? Time for some political science and economics. Lived in Detroit and Florida? Maybe try to live on the east and west coasts. I actually did all of these things, and it worked. While all of this diversification has not gained me one vote for national office, it has indeed prepared me for many other good things that have come my way.

"I may be the only person in the world who goes to the Caribbean for business and Detroit for vacation," I like to tell my friends. That, indeed, has been my wonderful road less traveled.

Editor's note: Dan's footnote cracked me up. When I asked him about it, he said the supervisor was actually wearing a raincoat and flashed it open and closed as he said the phrase "...expose yourself." Dan, a young and naïve

---

[1] This generally holds all along in one's life - as one of my first World Bank supervisors put it, the secret to success in the Bank is to "do good work and expose yourself."

intern at the time, knew little about sexual perversions or off-color jokes, and it took some time before he understood the connection. How many college kids could say that today?

Never Plead Guilty

Craig Cahoon, Attorney at Law

I have never met Craig Cahoon. His parents are neighbors and friends. Thus, I know he is from good State of Washington stock. Credentials? A bachelor's degree in computer science, an MBA, and a juris doctorate. He has defended thousands of clients on criminal cases in private practice and taken more than a hundred cases to trial. I needed a lawyer (to write) for this book. Craig had just released his own, entitled **What Do I Do Now?** *I asked if I could borrow a segment — giving him full credit, of course. He readily agreed. Finding it difficult to choose one chapter, this is a compilation of several, with high points from each. I was particularly interested in his legal advice to young people who party a little too hard and are arrested as a result. Every parent of a teenager will benefit from his words. So, too, anyone who finds him- or herself in a previously unimaginable predicament with the Law will do well to remember Craig's counsel.*

Supporting a loved one who is fighting a criminal charge can be one of the most stressful and frustrating times in your life, especially if you have no experience with the criminal court process yourself. It is hard to get basic advice about what to expect if you do not even know where to start.

I have been practicing law for over fifteen years, almost exclusively in the area of criminal defense. In that time I have handled more than two thousand cases, over one hundred of which went all the way through to trial; held countless motion hearings and had more meetings with clients and their families than I can count. My experience and knowledge will guide you and help you avoid much of the worry that comes along with not knowing what will happen or what you can do about it.

The examples here use the laws in Washington State where I practice. The laws in your state may be different. But there are some basic rules of thumb and information shared here that is useful to anyone who is awakened by that 2 a.m. phone call from the police telling you that they have your son or daughter (or friend or relative) in custody.

Just the Facts
At this stage, the exact nature of the criminal charge is unimportant. It's better to adopt a "just the facts" mentality. The normal questions are "What's the charge?" or "What happened?" Likewise, idle threats like "Don't do anything until I get there" hold no sway with the law. Put those reactionary demands on hold and stick to practical information like:

- Is the person ok?
- Where is the person now; and where is he or she being taken?
- Which law enforcement agency is processing this case?
- What is the case or incident number?
- What is the name and telephone number of the arresting officer?

- Was a vehicle involved? (If yes, find out if it will be left at the scene or towed. If left, where exactly is it? How long do you have to remove it before the vehicle is impounded? If towed, who towed it? The longer the car stays in the impound lot, the more expensive it will be to get out.)

Meanwhile, if the person is being held at the jail, make arrangements for a lawyer to get there as soon as possible. Attorneys have much greater access to someone in jail than you will. Find out as much information as you can. The Court System is incredibly slow, so you will have plenty of time to ask questions and find out what the options will be for resolving any troubles for the arrested party.

An arrest does not always mean a trip to jail. Depending on the circumstances, the police may release someone after arrest without taking them into custody. In this case, the person will most likely receive a citation, which is a written notice to appear in court. In that case, it is very important to show up on the stated date and time. Some crimes, like domestic violence, require mandatory arrest and jail by law. In less serious cases, the jail staff may administratively Book a suspect, and then release them almost immediately. Factors that come into play (and may be difficult to control if junior is intoxicated at the scene) are:

- How cooperative the person is
- Whether the law requires an arrest
- The seriousness of the charge
- Whether additional evidence might be obtained if the suspect is detained

Police get very experienced very quickly on how to get confessions out of people. The more an arrestee talks to an officer, the deeper he or she is likely to get themselves into trouble. Even seemingly innocent statements like, "I've done nothing wrong," can only serve to hurt the situation. Suspects cannot talk their way out of trouble but they *can* talk their way into a lot more, so it is best to politely choose not to make any statements.

Often the police will hold off on a formal arrest to give the suspect the illusion of freedom. NO attorney worth his salt would allow his or her client to make statements to the police. The police know this and have different strategies to gain confessions.

The Game
Some of the more common ploys used by experienced officers to obtain incriminating statements from suspects are: "This is your one shot to explain what happened" or that not talking "makes you look guilty" or "If you come clean, then I'll put in a good word with the Prosecutor." None of these statements are particularly true; rather they are part of the game played by police, with the goal of getting people to issue statements they will later regret.

Anyone who has ever watched a TV cop show (among the most classic, *Hill Street Blues* and *L.A. Law*) knows about the Good Cop/Bad Cop method. This may involve the same interviewer who starts out very nice, but becomes increasingly more aggressive as the interrogation continues. Or, the officer who begins the questioning will be kind and interested, insisting he only wants to hear "your side." After gaining a statement and gently looking for inconsistencies, a second officer comes in and aggressively interrogates the suspect, actively seeking evidence to obtain a conviction.

Miranda Rights legally must be read to every detainee before questioning. As heard on every cop show, they guarantee the right to remain silent, state anything you say can and will be used against you in court, and explain the constitutional right to an attorney. Another realistic scenario frequently played out in TV land is "I want to see a lawyer."

The law recognizes two different ways for a person in custody to keep quiet. The first is simply stating that no questions will be answered, the right to remain silent. By law, questioning must cease at this point. Further information obtained under questioning or duress is subject to suppression as evidence. The second is asking for a lawyer. Again, questioning must cease until an attorney is present. Be careful, however, because the law says that a suspect can waive, or give up, their right to remain silent by voluntarily starting to talk with the police after they have stopped asking questions.

I've heard many horror stories of clients spending six or eight hours in a tiny interrogation room answering questions by police officers. There is no reason to subject someone to this; have them ask for a lawyer.

And the Rest

The Arraignment is the first court date on a criminal case. A typical arraignment will cover notice of constitutional rights, notice of the charge against you, the release status, whether or not you will be getting an attorney, and whether you will choose a Bench or Jury Trial. In criminal cases, always ask for a Jury Trial. You can always switch to a Bench trial later, but not so the other way around.

When you go to court for an arraignment, be prepared to wait. In district and municipal courts there are typically dozens of cases that may be up for arraignment on any particular day. Most courts proceed alphabetically, so if your name starts later in the alphabet, be even more prepared to wait.

Generally speaking, it is a horrible idea to plead guilty at the beginning of a criminal case. Persons who believe they are not guilty will obviously plead Not Guilty. But what happens if they *are* guilty? *They still do not want to plead guilty at Arraignment.* Why? Two reasons: 1) When an attorney reviews your case, a defense may be discovered that you did not know about; and 2) even a person guilty of the crime can end up with a much lighter sentence if they have the attorney negotiate with the Prosecutor's office on their behalf (as seen commonly on shows like *Boston Legal* and *Harry's Law*.) By pleading Not Guilty at Arraignment, the defendant is asking for a chance to look at the evidence against them before making a final decision. Once a defendant pleads guilty, it is extremely difficult—if not impossible—to change that decision.

Many of us grew up learning if you do something wrong, admit it and take your lumps. As parents, we might think a night in jail will teach our underage child or troublemaker a lesson. The court system is more than willing to dish out lumps. Sentences imposed on even relatively small matters can take years to complete and be extremely expensive. A night in jail with a bunch of thugs for your son or daughter who is generally on the straight and narrow is not really the best form of *tough love*. I do not recommend it. Consider that convictions on a criminal record can haunt that person for years to come, affecting not just the person with the record but everyone around them. One mistake can mean lost employment opportunities, housing, and loss of rights like voting if one is forced to take the lumps.

As an example, here's a case of a thirty-five-year-old male who has never been in trouble with the law before. The police stop him because his car has a defective light over the rear license plate. During the contact, the police notice an odor of alcohol on his breath. When the man takes a breathalyzer test, he scores slightly above the legal limit. He is arrested for drunk driving.

If the defendant were to plead guilty to Driving Under the Influence in Washington State, he would: get a day in jail, have 364 days in prison hanging over his head if he does not comply with sentencing conditions, lose his license for three months, pay almost $900 in fines, undergo an evaluation to determine whether he requires treatment, do up to two years in alcohol rehab, attend a class about victims of drunk drivers, and be on probation for five years.

On the other hand, he could hire an attorney to defend him on the charge. With the facts in our example, the man would probably be offered a lesser crime, like Negligent Driving in the First Degree. If he pled guilty to the lesser charge, he would most likely not have to do any jail time or lose his license. Instead of being under court control for five years, he would only be on probation for two years.

As with any profession, there are lawyers who are really good and lawyers who are really bad. Most, if not all, public defenders are overworked. That is not to say that some are not devoted to their field; it just affects time available to the client and hampers access. When hiring a private counsel, cost is obviously the biggest hurdle. Again, there are good ones and bad ones, but private attorneys tend to have more time and offer easier access.

Use the free consultation to determine if the attorney is the right one for you. The basic three things to look for are communication, knowledge, and likeability. Do not confuse likeability with being a pushover. The most effective lawyers keep the lines of communication open with the Prosecutor while aggressively pursuing Motions and Trial. If done correctly, this combination creates a carrot-and-stick approach that obtains the best offers possible for the accused.

Every day in Court, I see people who just seem like they've given up on themselves. They end up pleading guilty to charges that I know darn well could have been reduced. They get sentenced much harder than they would have if they had fought more. Unfamiliar with the law, they make an error in defending themselves. There is no good reason for any of this. Exhaust every defense and every opportunity to make a bad situation better.

The Court System is slow and methodical. It is designed this way on purpose to ensure that decisions are well thought out and not made in haste. Your job is to keep a cool head and keep looking for options. Your loved one will be counting on you.

Of course, the filing of a criminal charge is a wake-up call, but it's what happens after the charge is over that makes all the difference. Find the underlying problem, investigate what went wrong, and fix it. "A stitch in time saves nine." We've all heard the finger-in-the-dyke story. Taking care of a problem before the dam breaks can save countless hours (or years) of worry and stress later.

Failing that, remember that a good lawyer will walk you through the process from start to finish, offering expertise the average person simply does not have.

Attorney Disclaimer: There are cases in the criminal justice system where pleading guilty is appropriate. The information presented here should not be considered formal legal advice. Any results discussed in this article were dependent on the facts of the individual case and will differ from case to case. This section from my book is intended to help adult defendants and their families avoid legal landmines and common mistakes.

Blueberry Hill

Peter Callow

Pete Callow and I worked together at Paramount Newscenter, an independent bookstore on a busy corner, a block from the State Capitol in Lansing, Michigan. There's something very lovable about Pete. He's decent, witty, hard-working, smart, and ready to take a stand. He loves dogs and fiddle music and kids. Despite the advancements of the Women's Movement in the Seventies, it was nice to have a man around when dealing with the odd-balls, malcontents, crazies, and street people who come with the territory when working in a downtown store. Weekdays it was all state workers and lawyers. Nights and weekends were another story. Pete handled everything with aplomb. Apart from the bookstore, he always liked the freedom of the country and the bounty of nature. He has found a way to incorporate that into his work and his home and his family and his life. Callow ended up working at his alma mater, Michigan State University, in the department they are most known for: Agriculture. I tracked him down after many years and asked if I could write about him for the book. He told me to make him look good.

Paramount Newscenter (or P-1 to insiders) was one of a small chain of independent bookstores located in the Lansing and Ann Arbor, Michigan areas during the 1970s and '80s. I had just been promoted to store manager of the downtown Lansing store. The shop was 5,000 square feet of books, magazines and Hallmark cards. Candy and tobacco surrounded the raised front counter, with two cash registers and small impulse items added to the array. A block from the state capitol, surrounded by office buildings, Lansing Community College, law offices and retail shops, the store did a noon-time rush hour to beat the band. Nights and weekends were dead except for a dwindling local population and a lot of street people, but upper management insisted we maintain the same hours of operation as our sister stores at various malls. We also had a smaller street-front store across from Michigan State University that showed better sales despite our impressive square footage.

Pete Callow was one of the book clerks at the store, and I walked into the office on my first day, replacing a beloved manager and surrounded by her closest friends. Pete stood out right away because he was nice, considerate, funny, and from Day One called me "Boss." He had names for the other staff, too: Trish the Dish, Coon Dog, and Mrs. Summers for the motherly and sociable woman who worked the register and opened every weekday morning at 7 a.m.

I ask him to recall the names we also had for the less-fortunates who made their way into the store on a regular basis, and he comes up with a virtual parade of personalities: D.C. (Disciple of Christ) McCracken, the Pope (plastic robe and cardboard miter), Michigan Slim (big fat guy who wore one pair of bib overalls all year long until Christmas, when his mom always gave him a new pair), and Chatty Cathy (need I say more?). He also remembered the Grave Digger (worked in the city cemetery) and his buddy Skip who lived at the shelter on Michigan Avenue; and Leroy Carson, a big lanky ex-con who was a real character.

There was an unusual situation in merchandizing in that, if our distributors wanted to receive tamer magazines like *Playboy* and *Penthouse*, they also had to sell much more offensive publications. Something about freedom of speech, according to the owner. Thus, each bookstore had an "Adult" (or "Adult Literature," which went a bit too far, don't you think?) section tucked in a back corner of the store, usually near Cooking and Art and as far away from the Children's section as possible. One of Pete's duties, never formally written in any job description, was chasing minors, perverts and thieves out of Porn (a name we were forbidden by management to use, but everyone did anyway). A thankless task to be sure, and I was particularly grateful to have Pete around to take care of it. Wiry red hair, short in stature, Pete was strong as could be and afraid of nothing. He possessed a certain style.

Living on a farm outside of Lansing in a township called Bath, the wholesome living, healthy eating, and down-home fun were just part of what Pete brought to P-1. Clogging (a dance with Appalachian and Scots-Irish roots that involves foot-stomping on a wooden box) and fiddling became a street show presented by housemates Frank, Dave, and Sue — all musicians — who would occasionally set up outside the store and entertain the lunch crowd, hopefully drawing them into the bookstore as well. He had pig roasts at his place that were like major farm festivals. A pig roasting in a smoky fire pit beneath the ground, barrels of cold water containing organic carrots or beer, tables of picnic salads, and square dancing next to bales of hay stacked in the barn. It was the aftermath of the peace and love movement, and everyone was getting back to nature.

Pete studied horticulture at MSU and earned a master's degree there after receiving his bachelor's in 1980. I lost track of him after that, finding him years later in the university's online directory. He became a research tech for the department where he earned his degrees. A picture of his old office in Anthony Hall looks like the common academic workplace: a glass-paned door, ceramic block walls, and a plain desk with formica top covered with books, papers and styrofoam coffee cups. Tornado emergency instructions, a calendar, and a photo of his son and daughter are affixed to the wall with green utility tape. Pete is writing in a notebook and looks happy as a lab rat with an endless supply of reward pellets.

He didn't finish his MS until '93, but in the meantime he married wife Mollie in 1985, bought a house and had two kids. They moved to Grand Ledge, a beautiful town west of Lansing known for its granite rock ledges and barn theatre, and lived in the country for a while. Eventually they moved into town to their present home, a unique place built in 1890, featuring a turret around the stairs.

Pete is still working at MSU in the Plant and Soil Science building on campus. Only now, he runs the lab and the greenhouse, and supervises the field operations. He works with blueberries and strawberries. I'm reminded of a professional bee, as he makes pollinations among interesting species of plants in the hope that they'll come up with a newer and better variety. The entire process can take years, at least five and often longer. I am fascinated to learn that Pete makes genetic maps for strawberry and other genomes. Apparently they've had some success and accomplished what this is all about at a research institution: bringing in revenue. This is especially important now that Michigan is offering less state operating dollars, a situation the department has dealt with for some time.

Years later, I am reacquainted with my old bookstore buddy when a mutual friend sends an article from the Lansing newspaper featuring none other than Mr. Pete Callow and the current research he is conducting under the tutelage of Professor James Hancock. The headline reads:

BLUEBERRIES ALONE WORTH $1M A YEAR TO UNIVERSITY

Apparently his new boss has developed and patented three new varieties of blueberries. Coming to fruition after two decades of research, several thousand acres of the beautiful berries—just the right size and Bingo! flavor—are now planted all over the world. They are one of the top royalty earners among the school's many inventions, which generate close to six million dollars per year for MSU.

On the day they get the story for this particular article, they have quotes from Hancock, but he's nowhere to be found for pictures. It's all Pete. Pictured in the office/lab at the Plant and Soil Science building on campus where he now works, he stands proudly in the greenhouse among the green-producing blueberry plants. This is gratifying to me because I can see he still looks the same, except for less hair on top and more on face, and also because I get the feeling *his* research was a big contributor to all this wealth, of which he shares no part. But it still goes to show that you never know where big money can be made.

I can't help it. Unbidden, the fifties song, "Blueberry Hill," comes to mind, and I hear Fats Domino singing about the thrill of young love and the still moon and finding a place where dreams come true. I think about the mysteries of fortune and the magic of life.

Blueberries...huh...

Editor's note: The song "Blueberry Hill" (music by Vincent Rose, lyrics by Al Lewis and Larry Stock) was written for the film The Singing Hill. *In the movie it was sung by Gene Autry, but was made popular by Glenn Miller and His Orchestra in 1956. And then Fats Domino sang it for true posterity. But for me, the teenage thrill of finding true love embodied in the song only really came alive when Richie Cunningham belted it out on a TV episode of* Happy Days.

Scoring Goals

Paul Castraberti

Paul Castraberti's Lemon Tree is a charming little eatery located on posh Ocean Drive in Vero Beach, Florida. Comfort and ease and a little conversation are provided by Paul himself during breakfast and lunch; wife Marybeth is hostess at dinner – which they don't even serve during the slow pace of summer. Still, they manage to feed 600 people a day in the 50-seat restaurant during season, doubling their business due to Paul's credo of friendly greeting, cleanliness, and consistently good food. It wasn't until sometime after lunching at the Lemon Tree on a regular basis that I also learned Paul has a daughter, Sophia, whom he adores; he is one of only five people in the Yale Hockey Hall of Fame (more on that later); and he learned the restaurant biz from his father. Arthur Castraberti (who passed away the summer before this went to print) was the patriarch of Prince, a little Italian place that started as a 12-seat pizzeria and became a 700-seat institution in Saugus, Mass, near Boston. Paul let his brother have that one. With the money made on the deal, Paul moved to Florida and took over the Lemon Tree, so he could do work he loves and still live like he's always on vacation.

Paul Castraberti was often in trouble as a kid. He was short (5 ft. 6 in.). He was Italian. Got into fights with the Irish boys. Didn't fit in. Skipped a lot of classes. Went to five different high schools. He jokes that he's been kicked out of some of the best prep schools in the country, and that includes Choate, alma mater of John F. Kennedy.

How do you turn something like that around? Paul believes everyone has a talent, and his was hockey. An All-American in high school, he was recruited by Yale and ended up captain of the hockey team. He was inducted into the Yale Hall of Fame, one of five hockey players with the distinction. Today he serves on the board of the Yale Hockey Association.

Keith Allain was a teammate of Paul's in the '70s and '80s, and now coaches the sport at Yale. Allain's tough drills, understanding of the game from a player's standpoint, and the addition of fun with something these guys love to do, have earned him the respect of the team. And also the honor of *New Haven Register* Sports Person of the Year for 2010. It's a distinctive approach from the more hard-line taken by their former coach, Tim Taylor, whom Castraberti reveres. He knows it was a different time and a different mentality (and a different personality). But Paul can't help but notice the difference. Allain brings out the passion of winning in his players, recognizing that hard work and fun are not mutually exclusive. Once his players understood that, they became a better hockey team. It strikes me that Paul Castraberti not only serves on the board; he learns from this and every experience. And becomes a better man.

New face masks were introduced during Paul's college hockey-playing days, and he suffered several concussions as players began to check higher. His advisor visited him in the hospital after the fourth concussion and told him, "You're supposed to leave here with a higher IQ than you came in with. You're done with hockey."

The day after a game with Princeton—in which Paul, who played forward, got one of those concussions—he had a history final. This meant the final two credits needed for graduation. He stared at the exam. Everything was fuzzy. John Blum, the quintessential Yale history professor, complete with tweed jacket and bow tie, presided over the exam. Paul walked up, explained the situation and asked to be excused. The deal was to turn in a final history paper and receive double credit to cover the exam. The request was granted.

A short time later, Paul went over to the locker room to suit up for the hockey game against Boston. No way was he going to miss playing them. The bus was waiting. The trainer said, "You're not playing." Castraberti replied, "I'm playing." Then, pleading, "It's Boston. I gotta play this game." Again, his request was granted.

Paul Castraberti is two points away from achieving a hockey scoring record for Yale. He shoots another goal at the Boston game and makes headlines in the student newspaper the next day. He turns in his paper, which he had written before the final exam anyway, for the history class. The proctor tells him a paper for double credit should be twice as long. That was not the deal, says Paul. He walks. Meanwhile, Professor Blum sees the hockey news, realizes his student left the exam the same day of the game, and gives him an F in the class. Paul goes through graduation and receives a blank scroll. No diploma.

Graduation weekend he got a phone call. His mother took the message from the Italian national hockey team, inviting him to play. Paul's response? "Ma, that's a prank call. Forget about it." He quickly learned that the offer was real, however, and five days later he was on a plane for Cortina, Italy, where he spent the next two years. (He scores!)

Cortina is a city near the Austro-Yugoslavian border. Castraberti starts in the Italian League and eventually qualifies for the Italian National team. Cortina makes it to the World Cup. In a game with the Germans (he thinks), Paul gives a sharp check to his opponent, wrapping the stick around the player's back and bringing him down on the ice. The player responds by spearing Paul with his stick (considered worse than fighting to the Italians in terms of foul play and penalties). Paul responds with a swift uppercut to the chin and draws blood. Immediately the call is made and he goes to the penalty box. He stands in the box (nowhere to sit), and people yell and throw stuff at him. Paul is shouting to the Italian ref, "*There's two people!*" Two people should be in the penalty box. Suddenly the signal is made for YOU ARE OUT OF THE GAME. "What the hell is going on?" Paul asks the coach. The coach explains that since he decided to call the game official *Stupido*, he was out of the game.

Paul removed his helmet, took off his jersey, and walked— again. The coach tried to tell him there was nothing he could do about the misunderstanding.

"Just give me the $13,000 you still owe me on my contract," Paul said, "and I'm outa here."

"Sue us for the money," came the reply.

In Italy? No way. So Paul stuffed every lira he could find into his shoes, afraid he would be stopped or arrested or worse as he tried to board a plane for the U.S. However, it was smooth skating, and these were the days when the shoes stayed on at the airport, so he made his escape. "Basically," he says, "I was kicked out of Italy."

Some twenty years later, Paul is serving on the Yale Hockey Board and the Alumni Association, and he's having dinner with his friend and dean of Yale, Richard Brodhead (since 2004, president of Duke). They are laughing about his experiences at the university, and when Brodhead learns of the diploma debacle, he first jokes about obtaining a fake certificate on line, but then turns serious. "Paul, you're two credits away from a

Yale degree. Take a class in anything and complete it, for god's sake."

The next semester Paul found himself on the campus of his alma mater taking a class to earn his diploma. When it was completed and the two final credits earned for a degree in American History, he returned home. Every one who showed up to congratulate him was wearing a T-shirt that said: YALE 1981-2002.

When he came back to the States after playing for the Italians, the years of working in the family business began. He married, had a daughter, and was caught in the madness of nights in the restaurant earning a living, missing the home life, increasingly dissatisfied. I have a real sense that as much as Paul loved his dad and brother, both of whom he worked with over his years in the Boston area, a man like him has a restless spirit. He needs time with people he loves. He needs to have more control over his life. He has to break away and start something on his own.

Now, Paul doesn't appear to be someone who deliberates a whole lot either. He is used to quick reactions, playing the game, surviving where he doesn't fit in, and taking risks. So he moves to Vero Beach and buys a house and has no idea what he is going to do; but he has a nice pay-out from the family business in Saugus and the deal with his brother, and can take time to see where life takes him. He looked into several different things. But the food business still appealed to him. Meanwhile, wife Marybeth completed the year teaching up north, and daughter Sophia finished out the school year. In the interests of family and returning to what he does best, Paul opened the Lemon Tree a short time after they arrived. (He scores!)

Some things you won't see in local articles or Yale hockey news items: Paul accepts as payment from a man with an undisclosed debt a weekly delivery of fabulous, sweet-smelling roses, placed in a lemon yellow bucket at the front counter of the restaurant. The debt is sizable, because roses have appeared each week for well over a year. Or maybe it's just worked out so well they've all lost count.

Another: I come in for lunch with my husband one day and comment how nice and clean the restaurant smells. "I like things to be clean," Paul responds, "so every summer when it's slow, we close for two weeks. The entire restaurant is cleaned from top to bottom. All appliances are pulled out from the wall in the kitchen. Floors are polished. Everything gets the once-over. And the staff gets a vacation."

Some of the waitresses and cooks have been at the Lemon Tree over twenty years. According to Paul, no one has ever called in sick since he's had the place. Locals know all the employees by name, and many customers are greeted by name as well. Paul always shakes my husband's hand, finds us a table fast even when busy, and occasionally sits down with us for a brief chat before he's needed elsewhere. He's doing *something* right!

Paul does not like to brag about his good works, but he does all kinds of additional things to serve the community and pay his good fortune forward and make a difference in the lives of those around him. Of course, he still makes the drive to the Boston area once in a while to visit family or attend a hockey game at Yale, which he does as often as he can manage. He loves his dogs and collecting vintage cars and living in the perpetual lemon light of Florida. And now he and his wife share a business together.

He knows the game's not over yet. But playing is much smoother now, and his skills are more refined. It's much easier to remember that work and fun are not mutually exclusive. If

Sophia has a lacrosse game or is in a play, he's there. She rides her bike to the Lemon Tree and visits. Marybeth would like a few more nights out, but home is good, too, and somehow it all works out. Everything is closer — work, school, family, home — and bigger than life. (And...GOAL!)

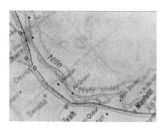

Footprints Along the Nile

Jack Claar

Jack Claar has all the right credentials you would expect from a learned, accomplished man who spent years in the halls of academia – and traveling the world – for the University of Illinois. He lists as his "grist for the mill" a PhD in agricultural economics from U of I, Director of the Cooperative Extension Service (an organization with over a hundred offices) for twenty years, Interim Dean for the College of Agriculture, and other assignments. He also directed INTERPAKS, an international consulting service on behalf of the university. But what hooked me was his work in Egypt. How much more timely could a topic be? Although Jack has been elected to the International Continuing Education Hall of Fame, and worked in twenty developing countries, I was more than happy when he chose to write about his experiences in Egypt. Jack and his wife, Charlotte, occasionally join us for dinner and I always find them intelligent, clever, and fun to be around. Watch all the CIA, U.S. Government, and war movies you like, but here's an example of the people behind the scenes who really shape this country and influence the world.

Working in the underdeveloped world has its risks and inconveniences as well as its rewards. In the risk and inconvenience arena, a few things come to mind. I think of the worn-out sagging mattresses in the hotel beds, probably the originals. And, as we were required to fly in and out on one of that country's airlines, I remember wondering if the same person maintained Somalia Airlines who looked after the noisy, clunky, sometimes-didn't-work air conditioner at the hotel.

Another Somalia anecdote will serve to indicate an additional risk. One day the U.S. embassy nurse stopped by and asked where we got our drinking water. We explained proudly that we were buying bottled water at the bar. She said she had observed bar employees refilling used bottles at the tap on the street for resale. She suggested we drink only beer or come to the embassy for our water. In short, underdeveloped countries are, well, underdeveloped and exposed one to an entire new set of risks. But the job was challenging and of great humanitarian value, so I struggled on to work in about twenty of them.

My work at the University of Illinois included statewide, college-wide, and multi-campus administrative assignments and it was none-too-varied to deal with the vagaries of what was to come.

The most frequent type of request was to help develop a project limited in scope for potential funding by the World Bank, the United States Agency for International Development, or the Food and Agriculture Organization of the United Nations. However, many were much more comprehensive, such as designing a college of agriculture in Iran shortly before the shah was deposed, the reorganization of the department of agriculture in Malta, setting up new agricultural colleges in Sierra Leone and India, and making a comprehensive study of agriculture in Egypt.

The Egypt venture I have chosen to highlight because it simply stands out. This was an opportunity for which one might wait a lifetime and one that had the potential to impact the future of that country. For me, Egypt has always been a most intriguing and downright mysterious place with its pyramid tombs, pharaohs, scarabs, and the inscrutable smile of the sphinx.

As generations of school children have known, Egypt was an *ever normal granary* for its neighbors in ancient times. With its irrigation and annual Nile flooding which brought large deposits of fertile soil, Egypt consistently produced good crops with very high yields per acre. This repute stretches back to ancient times when, according to Biblical lore, David's brothers, who had sold him into slavery, came to Egypt to negotiate for grain because of a failed crop in their homeland. To their utter amazement, they found their brother in a position of power to help them.

However now, centuries after serving faithfully for so many years, the Nile region was no longer functioning at its former high standard, with problems in both yields and income.

Soon after becoming president, in 1981 Mubarak asked President Reagan for a team of agricultural experts to make a comprehensive study of the situation and recommend changes. Reagan's response was to set up a Presidential Mission, and I was pleased to accept the assignment of deputy director.

The first step was to send an advance group of United States Department of Agriculture personnel to develop data that could be used for analysis and planning. Approximately six weeks later our team arrived. It was comprised of fifteen people, representing a wide array of disciplines from universities and government, who had extensive experience working in developing countries.

Early on, it became clear we were not dealing with solely technical problems but that overall agricultural policy and national priorities played central roles. Our work would be affected by many aspects of the *big picture.*

1. The expenditures of the Egyptian government were not bound by the economic output of the domestic economy for there were many other sources of income. Included were the

Suez Canal, oil in the Sinai, remittances paid by a large number of people working outside the country, and more than a billion dollars annually from the United States in military and economic aid. These sources of income allowed the national government to subsidize its domestic economy beyond what most countries could manage. For example, bread was so heavily subsidized it could be bought by the people for a penny a loaf.

2. Egypt had a very high birth rate. This created pressure for more housing, jobs, and food production. One of the lesser ways this impacted agriculture was that the fertile soil along the Nile was being used for making bricks to provide new houses for the burgeoning population. Not a great problem but one inching along day by day.

3. It was government policy to provide free education through two years of college and then guarantee employment in government agencies. This resulted in far too many employees without enough work to do. One department head told us he had half of his employees stay at home and simply draw their pay checks. Morale then improved since he now had enough work for the others and neither did he have to provide as much office space. (I presume the employees took turns working.)

Another policy played a central role. One of the most frequent approaches toward development in the underdeveloped world is to divert income from the most successful sectors to others. Egypt was diverting income from agriculture to urban development, even to starting entire new cities in the desert. A major mechanism for this was to require each farmer to raise a quota of the much-prized, long-staple cotton, then export it and pay farmers about half the money received. This practice was being overdone, and, when taken together with other detrimental policies, was a major causative factor in the decline of agriculture.

The team heard rumors of other unintended consequences of agricultural policy. Since cotton was no longer profitable enough for the farmers, they were using the fertilizer meant for the cotton on other crops. Also, since bread was subsidized by the government, they could buy it for a penny a loaf to feed their animals. In addition, livestock was one of the fastest growing production areas because livestock prices were not controlled. This situation resulted in less intensive land-use and did not provide the type of food being consumed by most Egyptians.

Another factor affecting land-use was that the United States, being awash in wheat, set up a program called PL480 that put wheat perpetually on sale in the world. Hence Egypt, a nation of wheat-eaters, produced very little of that crop

However, the biggest problems causing the declining agricultural output were government policies that reduced the profit in agriculture, thus setting an entire range of things into motion; and the deterioration of the irrigation and drainage system. This latter situation resulted in salinity of the soil. Because of shifting priorities, investments to maintain the system were not being made.

In order to make certain all bases were touched and inputs in these matters had been sought from the relevant Egyptians, liaison personnel were set up; and each day team members would indicate whom they needed to see the next day. The team would meet every Friday to share significant information and discuss recommendations being considered.

Eventually our group recommended comprehensive changes that involved reshaping national priorities for restoring agriculture to a position of importance. We presented these suggestions to President Mubarak and his staff, stressing how soon the population explosion would overwhelm agricultural production if nothing were done. We also said that, in our opinion, spending more money to improve production along the Nile would be a more effective way to produce more food than opening up new lands.   We were told that these were not options as there were political reasons for the new lands to go forward.

And so, our job was finished; and I felt confident that our recommendations, if followed, would cause Egypt's agriculture to be a more profitable and contributing sector. But as I packed to return home, I was haunted by the fact that the population was increasing faster than economic growth and employment opportunities. And I wondered what this might mean down the road. Recent events suggest my concerns were justified.

Sometimes as I wait to fall asleep at night I reflect upon these efforts to help. Unfortunately, there is a tendency for the host country to revert to its old ways when the foreign irritant, and his money, are gone. But great lasting things did sometimes happen; and I drift away, assured at least, that my footprints can be found in these countries, no matter how indistinct.

C'est la Vie

Jean-Claude Collinet

I first met Jean-Claude Collinet in the summer of 2010, when he visited the U.S. for the first time with his wife, Lucette, and two of his grandchildren. They were staying with my friend and former French teacher, Melissa. She was traveling by car from Washington, D.C. to Miami and wondered if she could stop and visit along the way. We greeted them at our home in the Blue Ridge Mountains of North Carolina, and again a few days later at our home in Vero Beach, Florida. It was a thrill to show them two such diverse areas of America, Melissa had a break, and we fell in love with the Collinets. They have sufficient things, but not an abundance. Still, they have an exuberance for life, and they share everything. After a visit to their home in France, I sought Jean-Claude's permission to write a piece for this book and he graciously agreed. Herewith, I offer the tale of a true Frenchman.

Jean-Claude wakes, as he does most every morning, in his bed in the timbered room, in the house on rue de Bruchhausen, in the village of Fere Champenoise, in the champagne region of France. He washes, shaves, and quickly dresses. Before he leaves for the *boulangerie* he kisses his wife of forty-eight years, Lucette, three times: each cheek and again for emphasis. It is a short walk to the village place and the bakery, where he purchases a *baguette*, *croissants*, and chocolate *pain*. Breakfast is the same each day, yet something he looks forward to: drinking strong *café au lait* from a large bowl, dipping the bread in the coffee (if it is day-old, the coffee revives it), enjoying the company of his wife.

For thirty years they have lived in this house together, raising daughters Muriel and Brigitte, taking in niece Sylvie when her parents passed away; now a gathering place for children and grandchildren, nieces and nephews and, rarely, friends like my husband and me. Granddaughter Marion often leaves school on Friday and takes the two-hour train from Metz to spend the weekend. She loves to be with them, and at fourteen she is a mixture of quiet affection, animated conversation, teenage petulance, and refuge sought in friends on facebook and calls on her iPhone.

Jean-Claude opens the curtains downstairs and leaves by the heavy wooden front door for the short walk to the *boulangerie*. The street has a wall of brick on each side, individual houses and garage doors attached together in one continuous row. Each has a portal in the center with two windows on each side and two up, many with window boxes planted with red geraniums. From the façades, one would guess they could each comfortably house two or three people. I am told they were built this way to save taxes, determined by how much street frontage the house occupies. But inside, the house goes on seemingly forever.

Living room with beamed ceiling and fireplace ("chimney"), dining room and kitchen, bath and laundry rooms are downstairs. Upstairs, there are five bedrooms. There is also a new modern bathroom with a rain-spigot shower, aqua glass bowl sink, and a cupboard with carved wooden grapes painted a dove gray. A skylight shows the promise of the day immediately upon entering. Jean-Claude had announced that if we visited he would build a bathroom for us, and he did. How could we refuse?

Outside, Lucette makes the best of a narrow yard. It is May, and the peach tree is bearing fruit, irises are in bloom, honeysuckle overflows, and roses spill over the shed. The laundry rack holds the day's wash, drying in the sun-soaked breeze. Beyond that, the remnants of an outbuilding, destroyed in a storm. Through the door on the other side, a small hill and another garden, with early lettuce, strawberries picked for dessert, peonies and poppies. The bird song is incredible. The sky is the intense blue brought by clean air and the freshness of each new day.

There is also a small *cave* where the Collinets store champagne from the region, wine for dinner (and lunch while we visit), and pickles and preserves from the garden. It is a simple life that my husband and I relish in, and are grateful to be a part of for a few short days.

When we all walk to the town square together, everyone greets the Collinets. We meet the police chief and he takes us on a tour of City Hall (*Hotel de Ville*—not to be confused with a hotel), leading us up a wide stairway to a vast room where conferences are held and marriages are performed. Next we visit the café, where the owner greets us wearing jeans, black shirt, an Aussie-style cowboy hat and boots. The men order a Stella Artois. The ladies have a glass of rosé. Marion sips an Orangina. Few cars pass through the square, and the mood is congenial and relaxed.

Jean-Claude is retired. He worked for a company that builds and repairs machinery. Often, he was sent out to troubleshoot, problem-solve, deal with clients, and maintain equipment. He considers himself in a class above farmers and below the suits. Thus, he is upset when one of his daughters marries a farmer and not surprised when it doesn't work out. In France there is no pension plan, at least from the company that employed Jean-Claude. Instead, the first 10,000 euros made each year are tax-free. Health care is provided by the government in France, though it is becoming increasingly more costly and cumbersome to continue. Food is expensive, but the freshest I've seen anywhere due to the small size of European countries and the speed with which products can be brought to market via truck and high-speed rail.

When we arrive, the Collinets speak no English. My husband speaks no French. I have studied the language for years, but am far from fluent. Young Marion wants to speak English and has been working hard to serve as a translator during the few days she joins us on our visit. But the wonderful thing is we all *want* to communicate. Jean-Claude is expressive, bold, and unafraid to make a mistake. He uses body language and pantomime to convey his thoughts. By the end of our stay, he has mastered several English phrases and, as we sit at their big wooden country table for our two-hour evening meal, *le dictionnaire, s'il vous plais* becomes the ritual request, passed like salt and pepper. I hand it over gently at first, but by the end of the week I am sending it across to him in a smooth slide, laughing.

Lucette is a gourmet cook who wears her heart on her sleeve. She is nurturing, sentimental, and stresses over the problems and concerns of her children and grandchildren like a mother hen. *Cluck, cluck, cluck!* But she is always gentle and kind, often with a tear in her blue eyes, wanting everyone to be taken care of and everything to be just so. In the kitchen she whips up delights like chicken in mushroom sauce, crabmeat frittata, ham and golden-fried potatoes; and a dessert of meringue floating in a lemony cream that my husband goes nuts over.

Jean-Claude served in the military, but due to fortunate timing, never saw active duty. My husband happened to buy a French war medal at a flea market in St. Paul de Vence a few years back. One night while the Collinets are visiting us in America the previous summer, he presents it to Jean-Claude with great fanfare after playing the French national anthem on the piano. It is a lighthearted moment, but I can tell Jean-Claude is moved by the gesture. When we visit them, I realize how much this levity is needed to balance the horrors of war. A photographer named Francois we meet on the train reminds us that France has been a battleground for centuries.

Every village has a cemetery and war memorial, and Fere Champenoise is no exception. Marion accompanies me. It is too painful, I think, for Jean-Claude and Lucette. Just up the street from their house and to the right is a tree-lined road. Next to it stands a field of *blé* (wheat for fodder) with poppies along the edge and the village church in the distance. Then we come to a huge cemetery, with row upon row of Christian crosses and Muslim symbols, headstones of those who died for France. The French flag flies. A large stone angel guards the entrance. Etched into the monument are the names of the men from the village who died, some family names listed three, four, seven times. Fathers and sons, husbands and friends, all lost from a small village in two great wars. At the bottom, a simple phrase: *SOUVENONS NOUS.* Remember us.

We come across a grave marker for Francia Arvois, but his military name is Commandant Barré. Apparently many men used aliases, particularly leaders, to protect their families. He was born in January 1915 and fought in the Second World War. Imprisoned for three years, he escaped in May 1944. He joined the Resistance. A short time later he was recognized and stopped by the Germans, again captured, tortured, then shot and killed. Francia Arvois died August 21, 1944, at the age of twenty-nine.

Jean-Claude is a Frenchman. He has served his country. He is a worker and a provider. He drives a Citroen. Hunting rifles hang on the wall. Though the women are strong and he is certainly outnumbered, he is the recognized head of the family. Modern concessions include a solitary leather chair and a large flat screen TV. The computer in the living room is primarily his domain. Food and wine are major components of what makes life worth living. Family makes it enjoyable, and good.

Like many of his fellow countrymen, he is not religious, and has some disdain for the Catholic Church in which he was raised. The French marry at the town hall. They make it legal. The church is an afterthought, used for rituals like baptisms and weddings and funerals, but not as an authority to take direction from or a place to visit each Sunday. Beautiful churches, cathedrals, abbeys and monasteries exist throughout France, viewed more as historical buildings than places of worship. As with many people who have rejected their faith, I find Jean-Claude to be a good and spiritual man, nonetheless. He perceives things, understands things, and knows things. He is often selfless. He gets it.

My husband, Richard, brings something out in Jean-Claude that apparently has lain dormant for a long time. His daughters are astounded at the transformation. We bring laughter to the house. Richard brings enthusiasm. He defers to Jean-Claude, seeks his opinion, asks his advice, and taps his knowledge. I translate when necessary, but for some reason—and despite failure to speak a word of each others' language—they understand one another. They talk about history and hunting and cars. They laugh together over nonsense. The discovery of a funny story or shared joke is repeated for days, always leading to another round of laughter. The more they drink the wine, the more they understand!

I am proud to know Jean-Claude Collinet. This is how the world changes. We walk in another man's shoes. We take the journey to and from difference. We pay 1.36 euros per liter of gas. At 3.78 liters per gallon and $1.80 to each euro, that's about $9.00 a gallon for gas. Perspective is gained.

The pace slows. Things are calmer here. On the day Marion and I return from our walk to the cemetery, we find a bee keeper on a ladder at the house next door, spraying a fragrant balm that smells like incense as he is surrounded by a gigantic swarm of bees. Apparently, they are being coaxed to move from their current location under the eaves. Marion walks through it all as if in a cloud, bees everywhere but simply disinterested in us. They follow the queen. I follow Marion, meekly, as we enter the garage door and quickly close it behind us. Not one bee follows. Jean-Claude is matter of fact. *C'est la vie!* Lucette has already closed the bedroom window upstairs. *Fermé la fenêtre!*

The greatest lesson I receive from Jean-Claude is the joy of the simple life. With fresh food, good wine, champagne and peach liquor for special times; flowers, family and friends, every day is a new day and all things are possible. It's too late for me to live in a small village with a church, a town hall, a café, a Saturday market, and two(!) *boulangeries*. But I can certainly implement this lesson into my own madcap life. The two bottles of champagne (white and pink) from the vineyards of Baillet (a family Lucette's sister married into), received as parting gifts, can only serve as reminders and add credence to my quest for the good life. *À Santé*, Jean-Claude Collinet!

It's a Puzzle

Bob David

Bob David is one of those harsh-sounding guys with a heart of gold. Or at least he's working on it. He readily admits he doesn't want to hear about God, dogs, or kids. Ironically, he lived in a Methodist church for a while. Just bought the building and moved in. A sign outside, should anyone see the steeple and wander in on a Sunday morning, said NO KIDS NO PETS NO TRUE BELIEVERS. I tend to think he is limiting his vision, but I understand how it came about. He is not sentimental. Once in a while, he admits he knows I like him and he likes me. But he refused to write anything about his actual love life, considering it No Man's Land. He enjoys fine restaurants, a good bottle of wine, and hosting dinner parties, especially if they're in New York City. Cool things about Bob: I met him when I was seventeen and he just got out of Vietnam. He was coping by doing a lot of drugs, but he was handsome as the devil and let me drive his Porsche — for about five minutes. I had a little trouble remembering to PUT IN THE CLUTCH. Eventually, Bob put some of the pieces together and lived a decent life after years of craziness. And started a puzzle company. Details below.

I was asked to write something about myself, so let's start.

Family
My father died when I was a baby and my memories of my mother begin and end with an odor of cigarettes and coffee. She died when I was a kid. I do remember she did protect me from the monster in the far corner of my room.

Military/Vietnam
Drugs, sex, and all the other army stuff that goes along with an eighteen-year-old child robotically doing what white-haired old men tell you to do. The first adult decision I made was to actively protest the war. I never found people wanting to degrade me personally because of my tour and most of the anti-war movement was filled with vets. When I was discharged, I left my uniform in the toilet at Fort Dix, N.J.

Education
Lots of schools. From Embry Riddle to Yale. I was so lucky to be able to be in school for as long as I was. The education was great, and it really was a place to make mistakes and to grow up, which took me a long time. Daytona Beach = flying and beach time. New Haven = ed sit (educational situation) time to educate myself and learn a few things. I still stay at the Yale Club when I'm in New York.

First Career/Commercial Pilot
It was a wonderful environment. Professional and respectful folks work throughout the industry. It taught me to respect the work; wearing a uniform and being in my twenties was also not bad for my dating. I should also say that I am a homebody, and

living in hotel rooms was unfulfilling. When I discussed leaving aviation, my wife said she was surprised I took so long to come to that conclusion. I needed a new career.

Now What?
It was time to leave all the cities that my work placed me in: Philadelphia, New York, Miami, Detroit, Chicago, and San Francisco. It sounds like a movie but we looked at a map, sold our second car to the driver of the Mayflower truck, and set out to find our home. It came down to three cities: Santa Fe, which did not have enough water; San Francisco (being from the East, we didn't want a California license plate); and Portland, Oregon. Portland won. What could I say? Beautiful, clean, very little crime and lots of educated people. Here is an example of the change: When I went to New York on a trip and turned on the TV in the hotel room and called home, I would say, "OK honey, the news is on here and last night seven people were gunned down by submachine guns," and she would say on the news in Oregon they were talking about killing sea lions because they ate too many salmon.

My Shrink
I was on the board of a film group in Portland, Oregon, and the mayor asked us to put together a short film to take to our sister city, Sapporo, Japan. Because of that project I was given a present from Japan. It was a wood *tangram* (a popular Chinese puzzle that consists of seven shapes that fit together to form a square). Being that I was a bum at the time and supporting myself with part-time teaching at our local community college, I took the wood *tangram* to an art school and asked them to make it out of clay. It was beautiful.

Fast forward: I believe everyone should have a shrink. In one of my sessions, the shrink said my life was puzzling, and since my personal life was going nowhere and I just got a divorce, I started a puzzle company. So after several careers, including commercial pilot, airline administrator, and academic, I did agree with my psychiatrist: life is truly puzzling. In a strange way, starting a puzzle company made sense. I took my ideas to woodworkers, metal smiths, and potters; and the results were beautifully crafted desktop games in artful packaging. It's hard to believe twenty-five years have passed and I still have designers and craftspeople concocting puzzles and games that drive people crazy.

God

Where to start. How about the first time I stayed in the pew at church and did not go up for communion? Being a mindless youth, I was brought up in a Catholic household and it was taken for granted if you lived in their house, you also were a Catholic and a Republican. The day I left was the day I stopped being a Catholic and a Republican. I find organized religion to be based on fear. "Believe in me and love me and obey me, or damnation." Wow. Not someone I want to follow.

I find it funny that God also looks like us. A patriarchal male. If I were a woman, I would be pissed. Wonder if he looked like a dinosaur during their time, and where was he during the previous billions of years? I'm not really into dogma, as you can tell. I could wish some folks to spend a few days in hell, but forever? Thinking about forever gives me a headache. And for those people who believe in the Immaculate Conception more than evolution, they have FOX News for their support group.

Now

As an older man I found myself going to Vegas for a tradeshow (the only reason you would find me in Vegas) and thinking, "Should I spend money on a hooker or a car service?" And the car service wins.

In order to be able to say no to people who ask for donations (what a tough job they have), my thought and support always go to:

> Planned Parenthood - education
> Amnesty International – justice
> Nature Conservancy – environment

Twenty-five years ago, after hours of drinking in a New York bar, the following was written about me by a girlfriend for a personal ad in the classified dating section:

"A totally undistinguished man with no discernible qualities seeks a woman for a lifetime of domestic bliss."

Bob is semi-retired, lives in Oregon, and still sells his puzzles in the U.S. and other countries.

L'Homme d'Affaires

Stéphane De Deurwaerder

This chapter is included because I wanted to add an international perspective, and to demonstrate the advantages of cooperation in business and industry. I also wanted to show what one man can do when politics, fierce competition, and the madness of modern day society are all pushed aside, and personality and being are allowed to emerge. Aside from all this, Stéphane De Deurwaerder is a fine person in his own right. Stéphane started as a business partner and has become a good family friend, along with his wife, Laurence, and children Nicolas and Anne-Lise. But initially it was only Stéphane, and it is my pleasure to tell you something about him here, and life for one man in the 21st century, in the country of Belgium.

Stéphane De Deurwaerder is a Belgian businessman (*homme d'affaires*). As with most prominent executives, he can be defined by many labels. On the professional level, he has an engineering license, is a machine designer and builder, owns a real estate business, consults with pharmaceutical companies about large, sophisticated, high-priced production systems, and speaks several languages. On an individual level, he is a maverick: independent, knowledgeable, capable and well-mannered, a pleasure to know.

Hurst Corporation (my husband's company of which I am VP) had been looking for just such a candidate to deal with compliance issues on machines built for the European market. In addition, the company wanted to find ways to conform to safety and operational standards on machines sold overseas without having to charge the VAT (Value Added Taxes). The VAT can be as high as 17%, which on a $60,000 machine would be around $10,000. Hurst Corp was also spending a great deal of time and expense on training and installation. They wanted to assemble low-cost machine components in Europe to avoid excessive taxes. For months they asked every European customer they came in contact with to recommend someone to represent them there.

After two years, the Senior Engineer at Baxter Lessines, in Belgium, called. At this location, Baxter is a production site specializing in medication delivery and bioscience, a distribution center in Europe, and a large administration building employing more than 1,500 staff. The engineer had hired Stéphane to bring a Hurst machine into European Union (EU) compliance. This generally involves changing the electrical system and mechanical parts to match the foreign system (as anyone who has tried to plug an electronic device purchased in the U.S. into an electrical outlet in Europe well knows). However, converting a machine is not as simple as using an adaptor plug on a hair dryer. Stéphane knew all the ins and outs of adapting the machine to EU standards. It sounded like he was our man. But first, we must conduct the Interview. Mr. Hurst and I determined that Paris would be a good place to meet with him.

Stéphane sweeps into the lobby of the Hotel Agora St. Germain and greets us with the enthusiasm and ease of a forty-ish executive on his way up. When I go to shake his hand I feel comfortable enough to offer a light kiss on the cheek, but he quickly adds one on the other cheek. "Both in France," he says simply. My husband has already conducted some business with Stéphane and likes him immediately. Tonight is for my approval. He strikes me as confident though a little reserved. His face is ruddy and outdoorsy. There is humor in his eyes and his voice. He kisses both cheeks. What's not to like?

Dinner is at a restaurant on the square, a short walk uphill. The weather is fine and we are seated at a table outside. The waitress is young and energetic, and in a purely French maneuver, is suddenly distracted by a man waiting on the cobblestone street who is certain she will drop everything and come to him. And she does! She takes our orders, runs over to the man, throws her arms around him for a lingering hug and a quick kiss, and it's back to work. This is so uniquely French that I can only laugh. The boss does not look askance. Our service does not suffer.

She brings Belgian beer for the men, wine for me. Steaks for the men, seafood pasta for me. An ice cream dessert for all three. My two companions talk business while I enjoy our surroundings. I am drawn into the conversation but happy to be ignored. There's plenty going on and the food is excellent. I am good at learning things about people, and I ask Stéphane a few questions about home and family and country. His answers are thoughtful and intelligent. He also has a way of saying "Yes" that sounds like "Jess" that I find both humorous and charming. Before the evening is out we all know it's a go. We have our rep in Europe.

The next time we meet is in Paris again. There is some business to conduct, but Stéphane is bringing his wife, Laurence, and the four of us will dine together. We actually return to the hilltop square and have dinner at the same *place*, only a restaurant next door to the one where we ate before. Just to mix things up a little and try some other cuisine. It's crowded but they squeeze us in at a table outside. It's early and it's still light. Laurence is an administrator at a health and social services agency, competent and bright, and true blue. She thinks her English is bad, but compared to my French she's an absolute linguist. After sharing aperitifs and appetizers and wine, the language flows anyway. We enjoy each other's company, and there is much easy conversation and laughter. And good food — we are in Paris, after all.

Now we are not only business partners, but friends as well. Stéphane visits us in Florida to learn about the machines, how to put them together, to see all of the component parts in one place, and to understand more about the corporation itself. He and my husband go fishing and boating on the Intracoastal estuaries and waterways. I take him on a tour of McKee Gardens. We all breakfast at an outdoor café on the beach. When asked what else he would like to see while visiting, he replies without hesitation, "The Space Center." Of course, being Florida residents, we have never been to the Space Center ourselves, so it will be a new experience for all of us.

On a perfect day in December without a cloud in the sky, our tickets are stamped to enter NASA, and we each receive a United States Space Program Badge. A "man" in a spacesuit hovers over the entrance. The badge allows entry into the rocket and Space Shuttle displays, the Kennedy Space Center, various museums, and a ride out to the shuttle launch at Cape Canaveral. The day is a photographer's dream. While the two men talk shop and science, I wander off to take pictures. The Rocket Garden is an incredible display of launchers and jet engines and well, *rockets*, pointing up toward the sky like giant flowers on a grassy and graveled expanse. We tour museums, we watch the moon landing in the I-Max theatre, eat lunch at a space café along with a zillion middle school students, and take the bus out to the Cape—which is awesome. (Security is tight and no private cars are allowed in areas beyond the entrance.)

The day is tiring but totally interesting, and I leave there proud to be an American, further emphasized by the fact that we are presenting this place to a foreign engineer. We actually get to go inside the Space Shuttle and walk around, which I find fascinating. There are original space capsules and retired rockets. Everything is gigantic. New advances and old history. Every space-related toy and bauble you can imagine in the shops. Ever mindful of his children and the family at home, whom he sorely misses, Stéphane snaps photos and purchases small gifts. The day is a great success.

A couple of years later it is Stéphane's turn to impress. We are guests at the De Deurwaerder home. It is early May and spring has tentatively come to Belgium, with cool gray windy days followed by glorious days of sun and outdoor dining and flowers everywhere. We visit the Iron Atom—literally a giant replica of an iron atom—and tour the inside, climbing up through connectors to electrons and protons via endless escalators leading to globe-shaped rooms. There are windows to view the city below. Actually called the Atomium and representing the unit cell of an iron crystal, it is a symbol of Belgian industry originally built for the 1958 Brussels World's Fair. After, we eat Italian food at a quiet spot found on a street lined with international restaurants.

The next day, Stéphane surprises us with a short drive to a destination unknown. We pull up to a white country house with a black shingled roof and shutters. The lawn is more like a small meadow, with tall grass, white spiked flowers, tulips and lavender. Wisteria spills over a bay window. Trees are covered in blossoms. We head up the gravel drive to the garage, also painted white, which is a complete workshop for the artist who lives there. He is a sculptor and potter. We are treated to a special tour. Stéphane and Laurence have commissioned him to make clay plaque replicas of the Mouscron town hall and a *parfumerie* built in 1694 as small mementos for us. The color and detail are exquisite. We are moved beyond words.

Laurence has stayed behind, and when we return to the house she has prepared a luncheon repast of ham, prosciutto and salami, breads from the local boulangerie, sausages, cheeses to die for, and chocolate (for breakfast too!). Another day we lunch outdoors in the springtime sun at a sophisticated restaurant across the street. For dinner, Laurence has prepared a huge quiche Lorraine that she pops in the oven when we arrive back from the day's excursion. She adds a green salad, bakery rolls and wine. It is all very pleasant.

Stéphane's house is a mix of clean modern lines, bright rooms, and traditional antique furniture and keepsakes. The garage is under the house. In back, a large building has been converted into an office and shop area where Stéphane does simple building, design and consulting work. Living in Europe, distances are smaller, and he easily travels in his Audi 3.2-liter-engine wagon to clients in Belgium, France, Germany, and the Netherlands (he speaks Flemish). He most always returns home for supper that same night.

During our visit we see a different Belgian city every day. In Bruge (or Bruges) we take a river ride with the De Deurwaerders, including Stéphane's parents who accompany us. Bruge is an old Dutch city, established around the 11th century, featuring many stone bridges and canals. The Provincial Court Building, a gothic white palace decked with medieval flags, sits kitty corner from the Bruge Belfry. In the ancient city of Tournai, we arrive to see a carnival in the marketplace, a magnificent town park, and the massive Cathedral of Notre Dame (they're all named *Notre Dame*) undergoing extensive renovations. On the third day we see Brussels, an impressive city of gothic architecture, beautiful statuary, and a shopping mall full of boutiques, Belgian lace and chocolate. Street performers in the main square again create a carnival atmosphere.

There is a lot written here about what we *do* but, through it all, Stéphane De Deurwaerder the man emerges. He is not trying to impress. For him, the house and business he has built, the good food, Belgian beer, his homeland and history are simply what *is*. Family ties are close and well maintained. A keen intellect, clever sense of humor, and the ability to create have served him well. He blushes easily in casual conversation, but remains strong and steadfast when it counts.

Americans cannot compete with the historical buildings and cities of Europe that are centuries old, nor can we seem to make consistently the good bread and amazing sandwiches available at any village patisserie there. They've got Peugeot and Mercedes and Ferrari. But we have enthusiasm and generosity that are unmatched. Our continued developments in technology, science and the arts are sparked by the innovation ignited by freedom. We've got the Corvette and the Cadillac and the Mustang. We make a pretty good hamburger and a great apple pie. Can you imagine the results of combining our efforts?

Spy Mission Gloves Off
and
Shipwreck off Madagascar
John P. (Jack) Downs

*How do you find adventure? What makes life exciting, real, pure? Jack Downs
was pushing the limits long before the bungee jumping, mountain climbing,
sky diving, and other thrill seekers out there today. He is an Eagle Scout. He is
an elk hunter. And in the following missive, we read of his adventures sailing
around the world. Though born and raised in Chicago, Jack is the
quintessential Irishman: lover of books and dogs, sentimental over family,
quick to anger, quicker to laugh, enjoys a glass of Jameson; he is a storyteller
and a poet (he once recited the entire Robert Service poem "The Squaw Man"
by heart and was not ashamed to choke up in the telling). Jack has always been
his own man, thus his business. The John P. Downs Co. Inc. allows him to do
what he has always loved: work on boats, yacht and ship fittings, custom
hardware, bow thrusters and anchor handling equipment. But it's his heart
and spirit that draw me: caring, witty, charming, strong, smart, and always
fascinating. When his wife, Mary, showed me a picture of a group of men
dressed in traditional Arab garb after Jack returned from a trip to the Middle
East with friend (and my husband) R.H., I pointed to one and said, "Now, he
looks like an interesting man." I didn't recognize him with the beard. It was
Jack. He wrote the two-stories-in-one that follow.*

Book Two, Chapter Eleven

R. H. returns from the Pierre, still in evening attire, gloves off

He was standing at the window looking down on the 200 West Street building. I joined him there. Poor slobs, if they only knew. Ya, if they only knew. It was then that the security flashers went off. We had been expecting it and now it was beginning.

R.H. moved back to his desk and faced the door, two TEC-9s on the blotter along with the Baby Nambu and the Webley-Vickers 50.80. I took up position off to the side, with my cocked and unlocked government model in a Tom Threepersons holster, my Airweight in a Lew Alessi ankle holster, and the big 11.25 lb. Ithaca Mag-10 "Roadblocker" trained on the door. I remember thinking how messy this could get.

Approximately four minutes had passed since the monitors had gone blank. They would be moving fast, and in fact we could see their every move in the secondary. The secondary had been installed by the Dutchman. R.H. brought him over from time to time for highly specialized jobs. They would have the codes for the 86th floor. R.H.'s floor. World headquarters for Hurst International.

When the intercom buzzer went off, I jumped a foot. We heard Cynthia in the outer office. Did they have her? The door opened slowly and Cynthia strolled in. Alone. What was she doing here? Don't worry guys, it's over. They never made it out of the elevator. We used the gas. Another of the Dutchman's final touches. My idea, actually, she said. They're sleeping like babies. They'll be choppered to Langley in a few minutes.

Then Cynthia got that look on her face and explained that she now had a really serious problem. She pointed her finger at me and said, *The jig is up. Where is your writing assignment, mister?*

Oh shit, what day is it? Oh shit, my writing assignment. Let's see here. . . It was the best of times, it was the worst of times. No, that's been done. How about: Whenever I find myself growing grim about the mouth; whenever it is a damp, drizzly November in my soul. . . No, no, that's been done too.

Actually, on a serious note now, it was Herman Melville who got me started on my adult journey in life. Melville, Conrad, London. These authors pointed the way to my personal inspiration.

In my college years, I thought about dropping out and joining the Navy at one point, but I stuck it out. After graduation, I enlisted in the Army. I was told that the Navy was not taking any more people, and being young, I took "No" for an answer. A word to the wise: never take "No" for an answer. Anyway, when I was discharged, honorably I am proud to say, I was back to the plan of going to sea. NOW, I was free and responsible only to myself.

I went to work to get my nest egg going, and at about that time I met Quen Cultra. We hit it off right away. He had just recently been separated from the Marine Corps and also had the dream of going to sea. Together, over the next fourteen months, we planned to build a boat and sail around the world. We worked as laborers on I-55 in Illinois. I worked with a paving crew, then as a carpenter with a piling cap form crew. We went to work at 4:30 in the morning. We drove fifty miles north to start, then ten miles west, then fifty miles south as the highway moved along. Quen and I were so tired that we could only work on the boat on the weekends.

We built the boat in a barnyard in Onarga, Illinois. Toward the fall, we quit the highway and worked on the boat seven days a week, hoping to launch and get south before the winter got too bad. We launched the *Quee Queg* on New Year's Day 1968. That night, the temperature went down to twenty-five degrees below zero, and for the first time in fifty-four years the Illinois River froze up. When the ice flows down river and packs up against the lock doors, the doors can't open and all river traffic stops. So now we had to get a crane to hoist the boat out and set it on the bank till spring.

That winter we both worked as much as we could. At night, we built the spars at a Chicago Park District boat shop. We launched the *Quee Queg* in late March and headed down the Illinois to the Mississippi. Every night we had to find a place to tie up. On April 3rd, we tied up at a gas dock in Memphis and left at dawn on the fourth. That night we found an outflow creek near Greenville, Mississippi, and pulled in out of the current, which was running about thirteen miles an hour.

The next morning at sunrise, we were arrested on suspicion in connection with the murder of Martin Luther King. Mirrored sunglasses, shotguns, megaphone. Come out with your hands up. You're in a heap of trouble, boy. The whole thing. At this time, there were three of us. Quen, myself, and David Bruce. David was a retired actor. He had made sixty or more movies with Warner Bros, quite a few with Errol Flynn. I heard the police chief ask him his name and in a puff of smoke David Bruce from Hollywood, California, became Andy McBroom from Kankakee, Illinois.

We were interrogated and released.

We rigged the boat in Port Isabel, Texas, sea-trialed and debugged, and finally set sail for good in October, heading for Cozumel, Mexico, and Hurricane Gladys. Hurricanes late in the season often come up through the Yucatan Straits. We were in the Yucatan Straits for the worst of it, and had to turn back north and run for about three days under bare poles till it passed. We were lucky. The center of the storm went more over the mainland of Cuba. That turned out to be the worst weather of the trip. When we arrived in Cozumel, David, who had been thrown out of his bunk and across the cabin several times, and had almost every cigarette doused with a face full of saltwater within seconds of lighting, announced his departure.

I must add that simultaneously, due to the shock of the waves hitting the side of the boat with such force, our ship's bell would ring out at precisely the same instant as the water hit David, adding a carnival-like affect which was hysterically funny. (Only in retrospect, of course.)

He had been a very good shipmate and friend. We had a lot of laughs together. I saw him on television years later. It was in a cop series with Lloyd Bridges called the *Joe Forrester Show*. David died of a heart attack on the set while making that very episode. His daughter, Mandy, used to come to Port Isabel to visit her dad while we were there… Amanda McBroom became an actress and songwriter. "The Rose" was one of her big hits, performed by Bette Midler and others.

From Cozumel we headed for the Panama Canal. We crossed the Pacific, stopping in the Galapagos, Marquesas, Tuamotos, Tahiti, Cook Islands, Samoa, Tonga, Fiji, New

Hebrides, Australia; then up through the Great Barrier Reef into the Arafura Sea and into the Indian Ocean, Indonesia, Coco Keelings, Mauritius.

We had been outbound from Mauritius for several days on a course for Durban, South Africa, when we were unknowingly set north in the Mozambique Current. This is like our Gulf Stream. About 3 a.m. I heard a sound and ran up on deck. There are certain sounds that are normal at sea and others that aren't okay. Waves crashing over rocks is one of the not-okay sounds. The next thing I knew, heavy water came through the cockpit and took me with it, and the boat sailed on. There was no catching up to the boat. I had to go with the flow.

These rocks were lying along the south coast of Madagascar, so I swam to Madagascar, reciting the Act of Contrition as I paddled along. A jerry jug had washed out with me and buoyed me up. I kept it ahead of me like a shield, when finally I was heaved through a huge rolling surf and into the shallows where I could finally touch the bottom, which was jagged rock. I crabbed along and clung to the bottom with each passing wave till I made it in.

Then I had to wade across a lagoon before reaching dry sand. I was sure I'd step on a sea urchin or get cut, but I made it without a scratch. My knees were knocking and my teeth were chattering and I was standing there on a starless night in the rain.

Oh yes, and I was naked.

I could do nothing till daylight. I thought I could see something looming ahead— some indistinct form—so I ran to the top of the dune, but there was nothing, so I buried myself in sand and waited for the dawn. I knew the crew would come looking for me when things calmed down.

The boat had miraculously managed to avoid the rocks. Pure luck, because the sloppy sea condition and light air would virtually eliminate steerage. The sails would slat but not fill and pull, and we had no engine. The rest of the crew, none of whom had met my fate and were still aboard, had gotten anchors down, and at dawn I could see the boat lifting dangerously with every breaking wave, the nylon anchor lines stretching like rubber bands. If the lines broke, the boat would be on the beach.

I was now waving from the beach, and Quen could see me from the boat and knew that I had made it. I took a stick and wrote the word "HELP" in the wet sandbank with an arrow. The boat was embayed. This means that until the wind shifts to a favorable direction, the boat is trapped. I felt sure that I could find a settlement or spot a motorboat and get back and tow the boat out. If the wind hauled around and they managed to sail out, they would find me along the beach. I ran along the top of the dune to get a better look, and I ran for a couple of hours. Then I saw two natives with spears who took off running when I ran down the dune toward them.

They finally stopped and I made myself understood with sign language, drawing in the sand, and French. They speak Malagash but many in Madagascar also speak French. They gave me an old tee shirt, which I put on upside down and tied in a knot around my waist. Seriously air-conditioned pants. We walked west along the beach for another couple of hours until we found more people at a water hole. I still had my jerry jug, and I remember filling it partially and drinking. Now the gasoline taste had a salty nuance. OK , what's next?

We continued west and came upon a fish camp. The fish were hanging to dry in the hot desert sun. The south coast of Madagascar is all desert. Now it was about noon, six hours since I left the boat. The native dugouts were hauled out on the beach.

The sea was too rough to launch and fish that day. I got the impression that the next real settlement was miles away but a "bus" was coming to pick up the fish and bring supplies. In patois and pidgin, anything with tires and an engine is a bus. At this point, someone started yelling and pointed to a distant white sail. It was the *Quee Queg* broad reaching down the coast, but maybe a mile or more out.

Everyone was excited and willing to help me. We lashed the outrigger onto one of the dugouts. These boats are about thirty feet long, and eight or ten of us picked up the boat and ran it through the surf. I was amazed that we didn't swamp it. We all paddled furiously trying to intercept my boat before it passed, but we were in the trough so much that despite my waving a large cloth, we were never seen. The *Quee* sailed out of sight. From time to time we picked up crew, and Don Travers had been with us ever since Fiji. Don had blond hair and Quen had dark hair, but I couldn't tell who was at the tiller so they were probably still a half mile away when they passed. When at sea, the land looks closer than it is, and I guess they thought they would be able to spot me. We were all terribly fatigued as well.

Well, no bus ever came and I started to hike down the beach, finally walking into an outpost called Faux Cap about 9 p.m. that night. There was a makeshift gendarmerie there and I was thankful for the help. I explained what had happened, and wrote it out in French with all the necessary information. There were three policemen.

There was no radio, but they had a military hand-crank-operated generator from which Morse code transmissions could be sent and received. We took turns sitting on a bicycle-like seat and cranking with both arms. We cranked and cranked and tapped out the message for two or three hours until receiving a reply from Fort Dauphine. The reply went something like this:

Why are you in Madagascar? It was at this point that the policemen's eyes widened and their jaws dropped as the white dude went completely postal and his howling of *Fucking Idiots!* could be heard for miles.

I have to say that they were helpful and kind and gave me clothes to wear. I remember so well the skin tight, black nylon shirt, the heavy-weight orange cordoroy trousers and the bright blue Bata flip flops. Don't ask me to explain haute couture, not here. On the other hand, when we drove into the "big town" they went into a brothel and made me wait in the car. So they weren't all that nice.

It took two days to get to Fort Dauphine. One day in the police Land Rover, and the next in the back of a stake-body flatbed truck loaded with people and gear, food, chickens, goats, and more of the same. I was taken to the jail when we arrived and released to the care of an American Lutheran missionary. I stayed at the mission for several days, wondering why no contact had been made with my boat. I felt sure they would make it to a port and find me through police channels.

Finally, I got the word that she never had made port but had been run down by the Greek freighter *Appolonia.* Another miracle: no one was hurt. The boat was dismasted but sustained very little damage. Even the masts, which were stepped on deck, were basically OK.

The ship stood by and maneuvered for five hours to get the boat in her lee. We had made lifting straps for her and these were fit, and with the ship's deck cranes she was bounced up the side and dropped onto a hatch, then taken back to Port Louie in Mauritius, where we had departed eleven days before. I flew up to Antananarivo and then to Mauritius. A kind Samaritan who had flown to Madagascar from Mauritius brought my passport and some money, and the U. S. Consul made sure I got it. I flew out to Mauritius the same day.

Repairs ensued and the *Quee Queg* was off again.

We left in 1968 and returned to the states in 1971. I had many adventures. This one was the most memorable. Quen and I went our separate ways. Don Travers went back to the South Pacific and married a girl from Tubuai in the Austral Islands. I went back to Chicago where I grew up, but soon left for Annapolis to help my uncle get his boat ready for the summer. I stayed there for six years, always involved with boats.

Some time in 1976, I decided to specialize in steel and aluminum boats, so I went to Hobart Brothers welding school in Troy, Ohio. When I finished four or five months later, my girl Mary and I moved to Fort Lauderdale, where we married and started our business and our family. Then the real adventures began. We have two wonderful children: Caitlin, now twenty-four and soon to be a registered nurse, and John T., who is a senior at the University of Central Florida in legal studies. Mary and I have been running our business now for thirty-four years.

One final note. In 2007, or thereabouts, I was in West Marine in Fort Lauderdale when I heard a familiar voice in the next aisle. I walked around and there was Quen. I didn't say anything. I just walked up to him and smiled. He didn't recognize me until I spoke, and then we both broke down and hugged each other. It had been thirty-six years. Quen came to our home for dinner that night and we had a great time. He had built another boat, a catamaran, and planned another circumnavigation. On January 9, 2009, he was lost at sea. The boat had capsized in heavy weather off the south coast of Madagascar.

Pub Crawl

Tim J. Faber

Tim J. Faber needs little introduction. I found him on Facebook via his wife Nicole's page (I recognized their baby from photos sent to us), and we reconnected after some time. Tim gave me the line that he was not a writer, too busy with work, and any energy left at the end of the day went to family. I thought it was important to have something about pubs and nightclubs and a night out of eat, drink and be merry in a book about men, so I agreed to write something for him. The following depicts a fine example of painting the town red in Toronto, Ontario. But it could speak for many good times on many nights for all those who happen to find themselves reading these pages. And here we represent the Canadian contingent as well, sorely needed somewhere in this collection, eh?

The scene is Toronto, Ontario, Canada. The year is 1999. It's summer. My husband and I are spending the weekend after driving up from Detroit for a mini-getaway. He has booked a nice hotel situated near the waterfront, close to shops and the Hockey Hall of Fame. We want to see the *Lion King*, but there are no tickets to be had according to the concierge, and scalpers are charging $200 apiece. This is twelve years ago. It's too much. It would probably be too much today.

What to do on a Saturday night? I don't really care to suggest old haunts I hit as a college student, when I'd hop in my '66 Mustang with a couple of friends, drive for five hours, stay in a fleabag hotel in Chinatown, and hang around Yonge Street and the University of Toronto. Once, after a night at a youth hostel, a neighbor guy who was with us suggested a priest he knew who lived in town and would probably put us up.

With no notice but a phone call, they were unbelievably hospitable. My friend Marie and I shared a room, while Mike (neighbor guy) and my brother were given a room down the hall. The Brothers ordered us pizza and Chinese food, which we ate in community and conversation. One of the best meals of my life. I never dreamed of combining the two take-outs before or again. But those were days gone by. Now, roughing it meant not making reservations. No, my husband and I had something a little bit more sophisticated in mind.

We thought to call Tim Faber, a Toronto rep who had done some work with my husband. Richard always called Tim the best salesman he ever had—in Canada anyway. Tim had attended our wedding party in Livonia, Michigan, in 1998. When he decided to propose to his lady love, Nicole Boudreau, he came to our house to pick up her engagement solitaire, purchased from a Jewish diamond merchant from Philadelphia. This was the same man who provided my betrothal and wedding rings.

Tim was home and delighted to receive our call. We asked for some suggestions for good places to go in Toronto to paint the town red. He insisted that the four of us get together so he and Nicole could show us a night on the town. We agreed to a time and place to meet.

Before I go any further, bear in mind that Tim is ten years younger than I am, I am ten years younger than Richard, and

Nicole is a few years younger than all of us. Could we keep up? No such thoughts entered as we set out, but we didn't know what was in store. Obviously, we lived to tell the tale.

First stop: a high-tech video palace complete with pinball, electronic games, air hockey, simulated driving (where I ran into fences and knocked off several cows) and skiing; and those cases full of stuffed animals and other junk you try to nab with mechanized grappling hooks. We started out together with our pile of tokens, but soon branched out on our own. Nicole is amazingly beautiful and was amazingly good at everything she played. Yup, pretty *and* smart. Nice, too. Tim was in his element, racking up points and generating electronic sounds with everything he touched. You could get beer there, too. After about an hour, it was time to move on.

Next, we went to a seafood place for oysters and wine, followed by dinner. The atmosphere was comfortable, with soft jazz in the background, tables and banquette-style booths on a couple of levels, waitresses serving drinks, and a sumptuous selection of appetizers and entrees. Summer days in Toronto are long; it was still light out and sunbeams shone through the windows. This was catch-up time. Tim was a charming host, Nicole was delightful, and we all enjoyed our meal, talking and joking while sharing a couple of bottles of wine. After settling the bill, it was on to Place Number 3.

Richard and I had left our car at the video arcade, and Tim was now driving the four of us about. We all hopped in and headed for a revolving nightclub on the umpteenth floor of a Toronto skyscraper. This place had a definite vibe, with pounding music and lots of young people sipping martinis, cosmos and blue angels. It was crowded and smoky (remember those days?). Light was fading to dusk. You could stay inside or go out on the balcony and watch the city lights come on. Stars appeared. We grabbed a cocktail and went outside to chat and take in the view. Night moved in like soft velvet. Tim and Nicole are good conversationalists with a keen Canadian sense of humor. Richard and I can hold our own. We were having a good time.

Inside, I am not particularly comfortable in the club scene and was ready to leave before anyone else, but kept it to myself. No one sat at tables; it was more like a big party where everyone stood and drank and mingled. A few danced. Our group talked for a while, but the noise level was not conducive to idle chitchat. I wandered. Caught some night air. Sipped my drink. Hunted out the others in our little party. Finally, someone suggested we clear out and I jumped at the invitation.

Stop number four was a tour of Tim and Nicole's place on Beaufort Road. It was one of those houses with a tall façade, not very wide but goes on forever to reach the back. Set high off the street, with several stairs climbing across the lawn to the front porch. A narrow double-trail driveway led to a small backyard and rear entrance. They had bought it for a song and were in the midst of renovations. Solid wood floors and cabinetry, fireplace, tiled baths, brass fixtures, crystal chandeliers — old stuff that only needed a little attention to become a showplace. They both knew what they were doing and were proud of their work. We loved seeing how young people could afford a house in an expensive city like Toronto, and what they could do with it. Tim dug out a bottle of French liquor and we sat around the fireplace, all warm and cozy.

It was late now. There was one more stop before the evening came to a close. Nicole was owner and manager of a franchised Irish pub and wanted us to see her *other* place. In Canada, as in Great Britain, pubs are gathering places in the neighborhood where people tend to know each other, families meet for good pub food, and regulars can be found on the same barstool most every night.

A short distance from the Faber home renovation project, the pub was still shaking when we arrived well after midnight. We found a booth near the bar and the guys ordered a beer. I switched to ice water. When the staff saw Nicole, they couldn't help but ask her a few questions. Soon she was behind the bar, talking with the manager on duty, and then in the kitchen checking on a supply order that hadn't arrived. Watching her, it was apparent that she was completely competent. Several customers greeted her. Her staff loved her.

Tim was easing out of sales and other work commitments and spending more time helping with the pub. Soon they added another. And a third. It was fascinating to see those two in action. Today, Tim is looking at opening a bar and restaurant with Nicole. On their own. No more managing for others. Entrepreneurial Spirit: it's the name of the game. Contractual obligations must be met. They will meet them, and then the sky's the limit. They sold the house on Beaufort Road and bought a larger one. Tim is now the father of three boys: Connor, Casey, and Calder (the C's are Irish and Nicole's idea, according to Tim). All of his energy goes into raising them. That's why *I'm* writing this.

Despite more alcohol than I normally consume, I will never forget that night in Toronto. At the close of the evening, after affectionate embraces and slaps on the back and promises to keep in touch, Tim posed a question: "So, are you up for more of the same tomorrow night?"

An Augustinian

Allan D. Fitzgerald, Order of Saint Augustine

In the cool and quiet that can only be found in a church, my husband and I gazed solemnly upon Michelangelo's Pieta as we waited at our established meeting point in St. Peter's Basilica for our rendezvous with Fr. Allan Fitzgerald, O.S.A. Tall and trim, he approached us a few minutes later with a confident stride, a man comfortable in his surroundings. Richard greeted an old friend, while I was introduced for the first time. Allan lived and worked in Rome for twelve years, teaching at the Augustinianum, a school dedicated to research and teaching Patristics (the study of the earliest writers of the Church within their cultural context). He also studied theology in Rome for four years, and spent 1968-1972 in Paris where he studied liturgy and wrote his dissertation. Each year he sends a Christmas letter to family and friends. The missive below is one such letter. It serves to illustrate the man he is, explains something about being an Augustinian friar, and demonstrates the crux of what Fr. Allan is striving to achieve in all things, personal, professional, and priestly.

Christmas 2010

Every year we solemnly celebrate this day which fulfills the prophecy, *Truth has sprung from the earth, and Justice has looked forth from heaven* (Ps 85:11) ... Truth, which holds the world together, has sprung from the earth so as to be carried in a woman's arms. Truth, which nourishes the happiness of the angels, has sprung from the earth so as to be fed at a human breast. Truth, which heaven is not big enough to hold, has sprung from the earth so as to be placed in a manger... Awake, humankind; God has become man for you.   ~ St. Augustine, *Sermon* 185, 1

It has been a year since I have communicated with most of you. That's something I need to change in 2011. When I used to return from Rome to spend some time, it was easy to connect and often to spend time with you because it was vacation. Now that I am back to stay, getting around to visit has been a challenge. I am still working my way into a new job and dealing with lots of new relationships—both at Villanova and in the parishes where I help out. But let me spend this time with you as we look forward to the next time there will be a chance to get together.

First of all, a few words about Advent 2010 ... Is it time? I have asked myself that question more than once. Are we finally beginning to see and to feel that our world, our country, our Church—even our own lives—are turning a corner? Will it be possible—in Advent 2015—to look back and say that my hope for greater unity, for greater civility, began to be felt in Advent

2010? I hope so, and Advent is all about hope. Maybe that is why
I want to say it *out loud* so that it's not just about *my* hope. What
then is the reason for that hope? (1 Peter 3:15)

I have been noticing that it is easier to tap into the less-than-
superficial desire in others: students, parishioners, colleagues,
brothers. People want to talk—and not just about sports and
weather. I find a longing, an insistent presence that just seems to
pop up as if from nowhere; a willingness to pay attention to
one's own spiritual need, to bring a human touch to a
conversation, even when busy, to be generous, even toward a
stranger. These things keep saying to me that God is there,
gracefully hidden, waiting to be noticed and appreciated. People
who give voice to their desires—it seems to me—make them
begin to happen, to be manifest. Or, as Augustine says, our
desire is our prayer: "When desire continues uninterrupted, so
does prayer."

People still ask me whether I miss Italy. No. The time I spent
in Italy was a really good time in my life; it stretched me through
the people I worked with and served. I do miss the good friends,
speaking their language and being challenged by difference. But
just as it was right to be there for a dozen years, so is it right for
me to be here now. In fact, I am still surprised by how *right* it
feels to be where I now am. The years in Italy helped me learn
how to enjoy what has been given to me—both then and now.

Over the summer, as a result of electing a new Augustinian
Provincial, I began to get to know two Augustinians better. Art
Johnson and Joseph Narog moved into the community, and Bill
Donnelly and Richard O'Leary moved out. Both went to
Massachusetts, but to different parishes. Those changes seem
like a bit of a shake-up; a way to keep all of us on our toes.
Although I lost two brothers and good friends (we began our
Augustinian journey together in 1960), I have once again been

given the chance to get to know and to be known by two more brothers ... a normal part of our Augustinian adventure!

In June I became full-time director of the Augustinian Institute. Since I did not want to leave the classroom altogether, I asked to be free to teach one course each semester. That proposal was welcomed and, this semester, I taught a graduate course on the thought of Saint Augustine. Good, interesting students (who were also interested!) and I can now look back on that class with pleasure (that it went so well) and joy (that I was able to learn too). Teaching at night (7:00-9:20) was not exactly something that I was looking forward to, but it turned out to be just fine. No one fell asleep—not even me.

The conversations that happened in the course of the semester have helped me see my job as the director of the Augustinian Institute more clearly. Since Villanova is an Augustinian university, an important part of my work as Director is to help to make that dimension of the mission of the University evident in practical and striking ways. That means that I have to *sell* the Augustinian spirit to professors, staff members, and administrators—many of whom have already bought in. If nothing else, the Augustinian spirit is all about working together as truth seekers, and to do so with thoughtful respect for one another. I guess that means that *doing* is not as important as doing it in *a way* that leads us toward the One who has given us so much. "I don't want anything to benefit me that does not also benefit you." (St. Augustine, *Sermon* 82, 15)

Each year I give you a few words about Clara.* How often you have, over the years, asked me about her, telling me that you continue to pray for her. I know that I am not alone in thanking you! When you pray for Clara—and for all the other good people who are incarcerated—please pray that they might all see through all the *stuff* around them and keep learning to be the good people they are. Prison can make that difficult, but it must not be seen as a place where people stop being human. Growth does happen there, too.

Clara has just finished courses in Nutrition and in Physics, doing very well in both. It seems that Piedmont College has decided to offer on-site courses at Fluvanna Prison after being absent for a couple of years. Clara took a creative writing course with them not long after she was sent there. That means that she will probably be able to take courses in person rather than by mail. Clara has also signed up for tutoring other inmates in college courses (and no longer in high school equivalency GED courses). It is great to see how good she has been at networking with others and speaking up about things that are worthwhile. Also, I just discovered that my administrative assistant has a stepson in prison. Please remember him — Carmelo — in your prayers as well.

A recent comment from the General of the Jesuits is worth repeating. Speaking about learning how to speak East Asian languages, he said: "I had to learn to speak always with great respect for the other person with whom I am speaking... it is not a matter of personal effort or acquiring some diplomatic skills; it is best learned by becoming aware of how comfortable and pleasant it is when...the person is more important than whatever ideas we might have about things."

"The second thing I had to learn through the years in Asia," he continued, "was to be more honest with my own doubts and insecurities. It is more real, and, consequently, more helpful in human interaction to let our ignorance and uncertainty show. There are very few things about which we know something. Speaking with such awareness opens up possibilities for others to help us, to instruct us, to contribute with their experience and knowledge where ours fall short. This simple fact does marvels for personal communication and smooth interaction."

Thus, in being the teacher, I am also the student. In giving the sermon, St. Augustine is my guide. In searching for the true source that is God, I find him in each individual.

Editor's note: Clara is the niece of Fr. Allan's brother-in-law. She was convicted of conspiring with a young man (diagnosed as schizophrenic) to kill her father. Since the hype about some apparently occult signs and the experience of the D.C. sniper was great at the time of the murder trial was great, Fr. Allan says that justice was not served. The killer (the young man) stated in his confession that – when he went to the house that night – he did not intend to kill her father. Since he pled guilty, his medical records were not admissible at the trial and the appeals in the State of Virginia were all unsuccessful. Clara received a 48-year sentence, which she is currently serving at Fluvanna Women's Correctional Facility in Virginia. She is now 26 and has served seven years in prison. Fr. Allan awaits the one appeal that has not been completed: to Padre Pio, a Capuchin priest from Italy who was canonized by Pope John Paul II in 2002. In other words, he awaits a miracle. He believes it will be successful, but the time frame is – like all such matters of faith – undetermined.

The Business of China

William E. (Bill) Gridley

Bill Gridley has been a family friend for years and a business associate of my husband's for longer still. He hails from Wisconsin; is smart, energetic, a terrific businessman, and an interesting person. He listens and considers another opinion. He learns from his mistakes. One night while sipping drinks on our lanai and talking about life, Bill quoted the Bible a couple of times. I jokingly asked him, "What are you, a Witness?" To which he replied simply, "Yes." That led to an interesting exchange! We have since met his wife, Vicki, a pretty woman and a lovely person. Both are articulate, laugh easily, and are enjoyable company. When they can sneak in a vacation, they especially like Hawaii, New York City, Florida, and the occasional cruise. When Bill decided to take his business to China, I was fascinated. In lieu of writing about himself, he agreed (finally) to an interview on this and other timely topics. We made a deal. That's how it's done in America.

Bill Gridley is a Type A personality. Friendly, outgoing, ambitious and hardworking, he always has the laptop available and the phone in hand, often at his ear as our conversation is interrupted by a call. But for this interview he turns the phone off—a good sign. We talk on the lanai of my home in Florida, where he is visiting for a vacation getaway with his wife, Vicki. I know it is the only way I will get something from him for this book, and I do want something for this book about doing business in China. They come at an inopportune time. My husband and I are leaving for France the same day they depart. I trade inconvenience for the chance to interview Bill. The deal is struck.

The first twenty minutes are spent with Bill setting up the background by describing the business climate in China and how it came about. China, apparently, has a different culture and a different way of doing business than in the United States. If Bill hears: *You do not understand; that is not the way we do things in China* one more time, he is seriously going to lose it. Not only because it is frustrating, but because Bill has built his career on finding ways around difficult issues and getting things accomplished. He is a doer. He does not say "No." He does not hear "No." He finds a way. This is not to say he doesn't listen. Bill constantly processes new information, hears another point of view, and seeks the lesson to be learned in any given situation.

The Chinese government owns all the land and has eminent domain for building and infrastructure. Since the Cultural Revolution, the government has privatized various areas in pockets to try capitalism. The areas are set up with an entire climate of business. Zones are created for economics and banking. The government lends the money to start the business. Foreigners can be partners or "best customers," eventually owning a majority of the business to facilitate growth, but they cannot buy the business.

Bill has worked the seacoast from Beijing (New York), Shanghai (Washington, D.C.), Shenzhen (inland) and Hong Kong (Florida), the states in parentheses being the comparable locations geographically in the U.S. Gridley cites price competition and ninety percent product quality vs. sixty percent U.S. as his reason for exploring business alternatives in China.

He sells aluminum products for marine applications through Vico Plastics, a company he owns and manages in Wisconsin. Through a website called Ali Baba, he found profiles for the specific tubing he makes, which led him to firms in China.

It was important to have an interpreter who understood both languages when traveling to meet with business contacts and in describing work at various factories and shops, to explain when something was wrong and how it should be fixed. When his passport was stolen and again when he was conned online ("shanghaied") out of $17,000, Bill made himself go through the police experience, using a translator from one of the local farms. When talking with the translator, the policemen used a common dialect, which was then translated for Bill. When the two cops spoke to each other, they used a different dialect.

"What are they saying?" Bill asked.

"I have no idea," the translator responded.

"What do you mean, you have no idea?"

And, like a Californian trying to understand two cops from Detroit's inner city, or the Louisiana Bayou or the Bronx, the policemen were using a dialect a Chinese man from another province could not decipher. This was the first lesson in Communication in China: Different Dialects Can Spell Trouble.

Eventually Bill found a man born in Taiwan, living in Wisconsin and educated at the University Wisconsin, Madison. John was someone who wanted to expand professionally, and he was offered a chance to be a liaison for Vico and start his own business in the process. John had a good grasp of the English and Chinese languages. Bill wanted to go to China and develop a personal business relationship with contacts there. To do this, he required someone with expertise in the culture, business practices, and languages of the two countries. It seemed like a good match.

John accompanied Bill on several trips to China, indispensable for everything from simple tasks (taxi rides, currency exchange, directions, restaurants, hotel accommodations) to more complex things (arguments, business negotiations, behavioral expectations, cultural nuances). What John lacked was good quality control and follow-through, two things Bill could not abide.

Next he found Selly. The Chinese often take Western names to work with Westerners. When Bill suggested to the woman that she must mean *Sally* the woman balked. "It is too late now," she explained. "Everyone already knows me as Selly."(When I key in the name, in fact, my computer dictionary tries to correct the misspelling to "Sally.") After several more trips, Bill hired Sam (no mistaking that spelling) to interpret, and had many successful trips with him.

This led to Communication Lesson 2: Sometimes You Have to Yell. One factory makes the components and another factory assembles the components and ships. The metal tubing used in marine applications (i.e., boats) was arriving damaged in shipping because the metal was soft and it wasn't being tested prior to shipping, nor was it being packed properly. Gridley created a PowerPoint presentation and video on how to palletize, shrink-wrap, and prepare corner packing to prevent damage in shipping. The components continued to arrive improperly packaged and subsequently unusable.

Bill looks younger than his fifty-seven years. He runs, he eats well, he stays in shape. Every once in a while he takes a vacation. He prides himself on being able to strike up a conversation and talk easily with anyone, anywhere. And he is prepared to go to the source if there is a problem. So he hopped on a plane and went to China to meet with Mr. Zhu at the packaging plant.

Arriving at the plant after a long flight, Bill was armed with an interpreter and prepared to do battle.

"Mr. Zhu, did you receive the PowerPoint presentation I prepared and sent?"

"Yes, Mr. Gridley!"

"And did you show it to your staff in the factory?"

"No, Mr. Gridley."

"Why not?"

"This is not necessary. Our work is very good."

The Chinese are polite to a fault. Everything is proper. Nothing is shown. No one wears their heart on their sleeve. By now, Bill has an understanding of this and decides anger, i.e., yelling, is a better strategy.

"Why do you disrespect me?" he booms. "I sent the video of how I want it done and that is how I want it done! I am paying you. You must meet my requirements!"

A discussion ensues on how pallets are obtained, how things are prepared for shipping, why products are arriving damaged, and what must be done to stop the waste. Finally, Bill asks for a pallet and saw, a staple gun and a hammer. It is about 95 degrees in the factory and humid. Bill is wearing a suit and tie. He gets down on his hands and knees, starts sawing, sawdust is flying, and he is showing them how it is to be done.

Mr. Zhu is in a bit of a panic.

"No, please do not do this work. We have a carpenter! We have a worker!"

Bill shouts, "No, I am doing this!"

In a brilliant strategy of drama, impatience, yelling, and the trouble to make a personal appearance, Bill at last gets his point across.

"Will you do this?" he asks.

And the response is, of course, yes. Now Bill wonders if it will last, and how long.

A third lesson in communication comes when Bill asks that the metal tubes be rolled on a marble table prior to shipping to ensure they are perfectly round and sans imperfection. Again, the factory manager insists their work is high quality and this step is unnecessary. Besides, he tells him, we do not have such a table. Bill goes out and finds one nearby. He takes a photo and returns. Oh yes, the manager assures him, they have such a table. After another return trip and no table and still no testing, Bill learns that the translator has been using the wrong tense. They *had* such a table. And thus, Communication Lesson 3: Talk and Tense Don't Necessarily Go Together.

During the interview, I begin to realize a couple of things about Bill Gridley. First, he is a top-notch communicator and a good businessman. Second, that being a Jehovah Witness has served him well, and he attributes his faith to saving him from self-destruction. He got into shady dealings with one of the major Swedish families in Wisconsin. He drank too much. In 1984 he declared bankruptcy. He and his wife separated; his four children wanted nothing to do with him. He left the faith. In a completely unselfish act, his father advised him to return to a religion he did not share, but could see what being a Witness did for his son. Here was fulfillment, happiness, and passion.

Actually, Bill is passionate about everything. He attributes his divorce attorney for seeing some spark that still existed between him and Vicki, and offering to negotiate a ceasefire with a few simple words: "Let's have a conversation." Vicki's lawyer was all about time and money and "let's get this over with."

A church elder asked a simple question: "Is it over?"

Bill responded, "I think it's over."

The church elder said, "If you *think* it's over, it's not over. If you *know* it's over, that's different. Do you think Vince Lombardi says to his team, behind in the fourth quarter, to go out there and do whatever they want because they're going to lose anyway? Bill, it's the fourth quarter. What do you want to do?"

Bill got his wife back, started Vico (named for her), returned to the faith they share, and began to earn the respect of his children again. A few grandchildren are added to the mix now. Lessons that have made him successful and stay balanced are to enjoy passion but temper it with listening, to forego blame, to let things go. Most of it's unimportant. Work is important, and family.

His favorite quote is one he thought up himself: *I don't learn very much when I'm talking.*

And those are words he lives by.

Omnia Causa Fiunt

John Hall

John Hall is a family friend and he wrote the story below. He was married to Sally and had two kids and had put the Franciscan part of his life pretty much behind him when I met him around the year 2000. John is all about the South, though he has traveled some and made a life for himself in the Midwest, settling in Ohio. His mom and dad owned a restaurant in Kentucky where they served deep-fried food and nothing but deep-fried food, right down to the breakfast bacon. They played the horses. I understand Mama Hall was dignified and proper, and a fine hostess. The rest of John's family is kind of a cast of characters. He has always tried to rise above whatever station he was assigned to in life. Instinctively, he knows there is more and reaches for higher ground. But that southern boy comes out once in a while, like the time he and Sally served crawdaddies for dinner cooked in a pound of butter and served with more of the same. Mmm, mmm!

Number four in a family of six. Born in Kentucky during the war. We had a garden, chickens, goats, dogs and a pony. My mother came from a strong Catholic background and my father converted to Catholicism after they married. Neither parent finished grade school because they had to work on the farms during the war. Times were hard and basic food items were rationed. My father worked several jobs and remodeled houses for a living. We were never without.

I attended Catholic grade school taught by the Sisters of Charity. By 1953, my dad and partner owned the local Miller Beer distributorship. In 1958, his partner embezzled and the business went under. My parents packed up four children and moved to Florida, where I finished high school taught by the Dominican Sisters of Adrian, Michigan.

Strong Catholic teaching in the '40s and '50s. Each family was expected to have one child in the service of the Church. One of my cousins had entered the Trappist Monastery in Bardstown, KY. Upon a visit in 1956, I was privileged to meet Fr. Louis (Thomas Merton), who was then the Novice Master. My cousin stayed there a few years and moved on to a less strict and more active Franciscan order in Cincinnati, Ohio. I stayed in communication with him and became interested in the Franciscan Brotherhood. Franciscan friars (Order of Friars Minor) do work other than priestly. I was not aware of this in my younger years. Some teach, farm, take up trades, cook, etc. I liked this idea as I was not drawn to the priesthood per se. Unknown to me at the time, religious orders were looking for brothers to handle the domestic duties of maintaining large monastery buildings, grounds and equipment.

After high school, I joined the Franciscans with the Province of St. John the Baptist in Cincinnati, Ohio. I took well to the brotherhood and the other thirty-five men who joined that same year. We formed a tight bond and I enjoyed the companionship as it was difficult to leave my family. The daily routine was: 5 a.m. prayer, silent breakfast, work, prayer, lunch, prayer, supper, prayer. Yes, we prayed at least five hours per day on wooden kneelers. My knees lost all of their hair and I still have knee problems. I lived and worked in Indiana, Michigan, and

Ohio. After eight years I made final vows. I took the vows of poverty, chastity and obedience with every intention of keeping them for the rest of my life.

I went to trade school in Michigan. Earned my Journeymen Electrician's license at age twenty-three by passing the test in one try. Unheard of, according to the inspector giving the test. I worked with Urban Renewal in Detroit, rebuilding and remodeling houses for poor people, working alongside the Jesuit brothers in the area. I was also on the staff for training new recruits for the Franciscan Brotherhood. I lived and worked at Duns Scotus College in Southfield, Michigan, a 300-bed theological seminary for the Franciscan priesthood. This monastery sat on two hundred acres of inspiring woodlands, fir trees and apple orchards; and had a beautiful chapel for ceremony, prayer and contemplation. I was very happy until things began to change.

I was transferred to the Mother House in Cincinnati. Ten priests lived there along with two brothers. Brother Dennis was the cook and porter. I was given a small list of domestic duties and asked to take care of the boilers in the winter. Yuk! After I finished working a few hours each day, I was free to do whatever I wanted. Very little structure and no strong community life. Most of the priests worked at the *St. Anthony Messenger* (the Order's religious publication), or were retired. No one was my age, and I was treated as a servant. I only lasted there about eight months. I kept thinking that I wanted to do something meaningful with my life. Of the thirty-five men who entered with me, only about fifteen were left.

During the early '60s and Vatican Two, thousands of religious men and women left the monasteries and convents in search of a more fulfilling life. I was transferred back to Michigan where I resumed many of my old duties. I kept thinking that I would be trapped in the basement of these big monasteries for the rest of my life. Doing what? For whom? Young men need some meaning in their life.

So after ten years, I left and went back to Kentucky. One hour before I left the building, I played "My Old Kentucky Home" on the church bell tower chimes. Leaving was extremely difficult. I had nightmares for years. I thought I would get married quickly but did not. I was thirty years old. Most of the women I met were divorced and had children. Believe it or not, the first eight women I met were named "Sue." Must have been a popular name!

So I purchased my first small house and car with the help of my mother, Mama Hall. The Franciscans only gave me $250 when I left, and I had very few clothes. I worked at the Hall family restaurant in Boonesboro, Kentucky, and did electrical work on the side for the next ten years. I enjoyed living close to my mom again, helping her and living on the banks of the Kentucky River. My dad passed away when I was in the monastery; however I was granted the request to spend time with him before the end.

All the time desiring to give of myself in some way, I decided to become a foster parent. I thought it would be easy to help raise one or two children if they were in school. I got one, then two, then three and they kept coming. I did not like to say no since there was such great need.

When I had six, the problems started. The teenage boys came from broken homes, parents who did not feed them, and most did not want to go to school. Some worked at Hall's Restaurant. Then one day it got to be too much for one person to handle and I gave it all up.

Shortly thereafter I met the love of my life. At thirty-five, I met a fine lady of the same age, Catholic, and her name was not

Sue. We met on a camping trip with mutual friends. She liked the same things I did: boating, fishing, hiking, camping and traveling. We both wanted kids. WOW! A perfect match. We dated for several years. Sally was well educated, drove a white Corvette, and had a great job. Christmas of 1979, I got up the courage to ask for her hand in marriage. She said yes and we married in April 1980.

Sally lived in Cincinnati, and we decided I should move and look for a job there. I printed a hundred resumes, called a head-hunter in Cincinnati and got an interview the first week. BOOM! I got a job with Kentucky Fried Chicken and only used one resume. I loved it since I had been eating KFC chicken all my life. We bought our first house in West Chester, Ohio.

In 1985, I got a big promotion and was transferred to Dallas, Texas. We lived in a suburb called Southlake. KFC, Pizza Hut and Taco Bell were spun off Pepsi to a new company called YUM! Brands. KFC sent me to London and Hawaii to set up maintenance programs for Operations.

With my years of eating KFC chicken while growing up in Kentucky, I was also able to identify problems with product quality. Just by entering a kitchen where it was cooking. I could tell by sense of smell if something wasn't right. My extensive experience on cooking equipment helped identify BTU issues with the cookers in other countries that actually changed the flavor of the chicken. When I discovered the difference and why, it could easily be fixed. I had many promotions over twenty-five years and retired at age sixty-two.

Life in Texas brought many surprises. Intense sun, blowing dust, hail storms and tornados. Big hats and snakeskin boots. Sally became a politician. I managed 350 facilities for KFC.

But the biggest surprise came one day while getting a haircut. My hairdresser mentioned that she had adopted a child through her church, and I expressed an interest in adoption. About six months later, the hairdresser called to see if we were still interested. Her church was looking for a home for a child. The young boy was six years old and we were reluctant. She suggested we have him over for the weekend to see if it was a good match. Sally and I were very excited to try this. Bob came that weekend and never left. About two years later, we were able to adopt his sister. We were very happy and had a great family. Bob and Jen have now grown up to be responsible adults and we have a granddaughter. We all live close together and continue to enjoy life. Bob and Jennifer are proud members of the Choctaw Tribe of Oklahoma, with full voting rights.

My parents gave me great direction and then left me alone to grow. I have lived in six states, had a successful career, married a wonderful person and have great children. What more can a man ask for?

I still have my Dispensation from Vows signed by the Pope. However, it was written in Latin and I am not sure exactly what it says, but I know for sure that I am not going back to the Monastery.

Omnia causa fiunt

I *can* tell you what that says because it suits my life perfectly: "All things happen for a reason."

Graphic Designs

Brian Holmes

I met Brian Holmes only recently, but I liked him right away. He not only helped design the cover, but agreed to be interviewed to be part of the book. His full name is Dwight Brian Holmes, but he generally skips the first name he shares with his dad, and goes by "Brian." At thirty-nine years, he has acquired an education, married, made a family, and created a business for himself that continually changes to suit budding interests and concerns. He develops new ideas and knows how to make them happen. Beyond business, Brian is a compassionate man, with a wry sense of humor that quickly dispels tension, and a perceptiveness and understanding that help enormously with the problems of the day. He and his wife, Wendy (another delightful person), laugh at their foibles and share everything and find solutions together. Perhaps that's why they have a marriage that works. In his spare time he rides a Ducati. Oh, another thing: Brian is totally into graphic arts, pinstriping on cars and motorcycles, and cool sign- making. How fun is that?

On a hot sunny day in April, after a short flight from Miami, Wendy and Brian Holmes arrive in Guatemala. They land in Guatemala City, the capital, so the airport itself is fairly modern and even under construction for improvements. Still, they emerge from customs and exit the airport to see hundreds of people standing on a dusty road, waiting for family members.

They are not on vacation. A baby awaits them. Diego is six weeks old, consciously unaware that a couple in the United States is ready, willing, and able to care for him and love him and make him their own. And yet, surely he is aware on some physical and spiritual level of the need for something more. During the months leading up to the adoption, Diego lives with a foster family in Guatemala. Brian and Wendy provide them with a disposable camera so they can take pictures; and bring the camera back after their visits and develop the film. In one, the baby is being bathed in a big blue plastic pail. He is smiling and covered in soap suds. In another, he sleeps on a ragged sofa with chairs across the edge so he won't fall. He is loved by the foster mother, and she cries on the day she has to part with him. Mr. and Mrs. Holmes first see Diego on that April 2006 visit and, after three or four more visits, bring him home to the United States. It is the day before Diego's first birthday.

There are other factors involved leading up to this homecoming. Wendy wants a foreign child to have the opportunity to live in the U.S. It is her wish to adopt. Korea and Russia and China are faraway places with loads of red tape and travel time required. Brian has his own business and cannot take weeks or months in pursuit of a child. They have investigated adopting an American baby and have given up. They don't want to engage in the years of waiting and hoping, paperwork and approvals necessary to surmount the American adoption system. There is also a U.S. law stating that the biological parents may seek to reclaim their child until he or she reaches the age of eighteen. This is not a question they wish to have looming over them. So, together they settle on Guatemala.

Brian thinks surely they are guided by an entity beyond themselves, as they stumble upon an agency in Fort Pierce, Florida, just southeast of where they live in Vero Beach. After conducting the initial interview, the agency refers them to a law firm that deals with immigration and adoptions. They are honest and legitimate, the staff helpful and kind, and the process runs smoothly. After months of meetings with the attorneys, and several visits to Guatemala, Brian and his wife have finally adopted a baby.

It is not that the couple cannot have a child together. Wendy, an attractive young woman with brown eyes and long hair she fixes in soft waves, is perfectly healthy. But she is both noble and adamant in her insistence that many children are born who have nothing and no one; she knows there is a child out there who needs someone just like them. Brian has dark hair and hazel eyes. He shaves before his interview with me, but his beard is almost growing before my eyes as we talk together! Wendy loves the dark straight hair and the dark eyes and the bright faces of this Central American people. They are physical characteristics shared by her husband, though his ancestry is English and German. (Brian's ancestry can be traced through the Holmes line to Richard Warren, who came on the *Mayflower*.)

The new parents were concerned about the conditions in which Diego spent his first months, but they knew what they had to give. They were sure love would overcome all obstacles. They did everything to expedite the process. The appointment with the U.S. Embassy was set up for a week later than Diego's first birthday, which would've meant another week in Guatemala City before they could bring Diego home. Pulling out all the stops, they asked Wendy's dad, a career National Security Administration (NSA) man, to type an "official letter" stating that the appointment must be moved up because Brian needed to return and run his business. In Central America, they do not necessarily respond to American government letters and instructions (as evidenced by the Hollywood V.I.P. who obtained an official letter of reference from President Clinton in order to bump ahead in the process and was refused). Nonetheless, a career government employee seemed the best person to write on their behalf, and the request was granted.

Diego was the perfect baby. Quiet, content, and he was sleeping through the night. He showed early signs of intelligence, responding to stimuli, following the movements of his parents with his eyes. As he grew to become a toddler, the parents began to see small signs of concern. He had trouble eating and liked only a few foods. He had balance problems and appeared more clumsy than normal. The simplest tools were difficult for Diego, like handling scissors or dressing himself. Writing was laborious, as was the use of crayons and silverware. Finally, a preschool psychologist noted Diego's constant pulling at his clothing. Sensitivity to tags on shirts and seams in clothing is a classic symptom of Sensory Processing Disorder or SPD. After a physician examined Diego, he referred them to an occupational therapist, who reaffirmed the psychologist's observations and confirmed the diagnosis.

Brian and Wendy went through the classic doubts and fears, asking themselves the usual questions: Did we do something wrong? Was this caused by Diego's first few months in Guatemala, with poor conditions and lack of stimuli? Will he have this for the rest of his life? How can we help our son? What are the treatment options? The answers were not found in medication for A.D.D., and the child was determined to not have autism though there are some similarities. The answers, and subsequent treatment options, were to be found in occupational therapy.

SPD is a neurological disorder where messages from the senses are not processed properly into appropriate motor and behavioral responses. It is the brain's inability to use information coming through the senses in an organized and effective way. This can affect receiving, interpreting and combining information, as well as deciding on or executing appropriate responses. As a result, the child may experience motor clumsiness, behavioral problems, anxiety, depression, learning difficulties and other problems if symptoms go untreated. Brian was willing to do whatever it took to help his son. Wendy was doing the bookkeeping for the family business, but was also committed to devoting her energies to Diego. Learning and healing began.

In the meantime, other things were happening. Two-and-a-half years after they brought Diego home, Brian became the proud father of another son, Oakley. At times a chip off the old block of his father, at others possessing a look or expression just like his mother, Oakley was a true delight to his parents.

What was Diego's first reaction to the new baby? *Put him back.* This initial attitude was a typical, wonderful, charming child's reaction—not terribly unusual when a new sibling is brought home. But mom and dad continually stressed that their sons were brothers, their love for Diego was steadfast, and their desire for a strong family true. This led to a couple of results: One, Oakley is easily influenced by his big brother and may react to frustration or stimulation by screaming, running down the hall with a pair of underwear on his head (causing Wendy to give up on laundry and collapse in laughter), and other antics; and two, Diego is reassured and recognizes that his task is to be the big brother, a role that will not change.

So, while there are triggers for various behaviors that can be exacerbated by two boys three-and-a-half years apart in age, these good and patient parents have taken the steps to deal with them. Diego is engaged in occupational therapy, learning skills like how to try new foods, balance, write, verbalize; and deal with everyday matters like transitions, not touching things without asking, and being patient. His intellect well exceeds his age, but his emotional level sometimes matches that of a two-year-old. Oakley has helped immensely with Diego's emotional growth. Thus, the brothers influence one another. At the same time, Oakley is emerging as an individual personality: fearless, stage-diving (off the beds), athletic; a boy who loves animals and motorcycles—just like his daddy.

Brian has a Ducati motorcycle that is a sight to behold and a joy to ride and Oakley is enthralled. Brian's parents did not want him to have a motorcycle when he was younger. Around the year 2000, Wendy mentioned that she would like to get her motorcycle endorsement, which Brian immediately took as an opportunity (a sign!) to obtain his motorcycle license. Wendy never ended up pursuing hers. To this day, Brian loves the rumbling noise of the Ducati, and that's why he chose the one he did. But I digress...

It was Brian's idea to make this primarily about Diego. I sense that it makes him both proud and humble to talk about the adoption, an event bigger than concerns of self. The challenges are enormous. But the rewards are great, too. Still, his background merits mention, and his story led him to this place.

Brian grew up going back and forth between Maryland and California. His father, curiously, like Wendy's father, also worked for the National Security Administration (NSA), but did not spend his career there. He had always wanted to be in the space business and was soon hired by Cal Tech at their jet propulsion lab. Dad also had several one-year positions in

Washington, D.C., working for NASA. Thus, the homes on both coasts. In the early '80s, Brian started traveling to Florida to visit his grandparents, and always felt as though he had another home there.

He attended Elon College (University since 2001), a private liberal arts school in North Carolina, where he spent only one semester. Wendy was at the University of Maryland, Baltimore County. They had met in high school in Maryland, introduced by a friend. And Brian missed her. So he transferred to UMBC, where he could be close to Wendy and major in Art/Design, neither of which he could do at Elon. There he studied graphic design and computer animation. They married in 1994 and graduated in 1995. During that time, they worked the 10 p.m. to 7 a.m. shift at a grocery store and went to school during the day. They liked it well enough, but eventually began thinking about day jobs.

Brian had every intention of using his talent and skills to work in the film industry, specializing in commercials. It was Wendy who saw an ad for a sign company headquartered in Columbia, Md. They were a franchise. This was not the direction Brian had planned to take, but he interviewed and was hired. He approached them with the idea of opening a shop in Vero Beach, Florida. Management was enthused about the suggestion and gave him the go-ahead. And suddenly Brian was directing his own destiny!

In January 1996 they made the move, opened Signs by Tomorrow, and formed DBH Graphics & Fine Arts, Inc. Computers were just taking over. Everyone was still using vinyl graphics, which Brian was very good at. He also loved hand-painted lettering and designs. When he saw an article in *SignCraft* magazine featuring a sample panel of pinstriping on a wall in a shop, he went nuts. He wanted to see more. This was for him. When someone asked him if he could do that sort of thing, he immediately said yes. The first job led to referrals. It just took off from there.

Pinstriping is a process of painting symmetrical lines with a sword striper brush (made of squirrel hair), primarily on cars and motorcycles. Influenced by the artwork of graphic artists and fathers of the California *Kustom Kulture* like Ed Roth (cartoonist, artist, custom car builder and creator of the hot-rod icon, Rat Fink) and Kenneth Howard aka Von Dutch (motorcycle mechanic, metal fabricator, artist and pinstriper, whose famous works include the flying eyeball), the expression saw its heyday in the '50s and '60s, and was making a comeback. The designs are all hand-painted, but not just striping—this art also involves cartoon characters, specialty painting, counter-culture designs, gold leaf, and other graphics.

Holmes picked up his first striping brush in 1997 and developed a real expertise by 2005. He loved the process of taking a design and making it symmetrical. He had the steady hand and the artistic eye to reproduce a design entirely by hand. He also became adept at computer graphics programs. The business used his finest skills and incorporated his philosophy of flying by the seat of your pants. To the consternation of his parents, his entire life is about *just diving in*.

Today Brian Holmes is somewhat disillusioned by the sign business, the problems that come with the territory when you hire employees, and the rivalry of inexperienced graphic artists in an industry where no degree or license is required and anyone can compete. Still, he knows where his talents lie, and he is already branching out into other venues that are challenging and meaningful—and money-making. His goal was to know what he really wanted to do by the time he turned 40, which gave him until September 2011. He is satisfied that the goal has been met.

Recently, America celebrated another Independence Day. On this Fourth of July, Brian and Wendy took the boys out on a small pleasure boat and headed for the Indian River, part of the Intracoastal Waterway that flows through Vero Beach. The holiday is especially fun and poignant because Diego is a U.S. citizen, enjoying the blessings America allows. Fireworks were starting at 9 p.m. off the point at Veterans Memorial Island. Boats arrived early, packed with picnic baskets and coolers, lining up along the orange-ball buoy markers afloat a safe distance from the island.

He wasn't sure how the boys would react. Oakley had heard some preliminary fireworks in the neighborhood the night before and was frightened by them. With Diego, he never knew.

Darkness fell by 9 p.m., and the first firework was launched. It was a spectacular display, loaded with pizzazz and the symmetry of pattern Brian so loved. Oakley had been asleep for some time. Diego had the time of his life, shouting in delight with each burst of color, calling out his favorites among the sparklers, twizzlers, Roman candles, and chrysanthemums, each one an amazing show of exploding color, lighting up the night.

Brian gave Wendy a squeeze, and wondered if it wasn't all by design.

Editor's note: Illustration for this story created by Brian Holmes.

Saturday Night in Texas

Gene Hull

This is a long tale and it may be a tall one, but I've known Gene Hull for a while and I happen to believe that it's all true. Gene has been a jazz musician most of his life, has played with a lot of the greats, and is still one of the hippest cats I know. This is a chapter (cut version) from his book on adventures in the big band biz, Chasing the Muse: A Life in Music and Show Business. *I'll keep this short so you can get right to it. Prepare yourself for a wild ride. Y'all enjoy.*

"Remember guys, it'll probably be the same tonight as it always is here. So be ready when the time comes." Tex Beneke was standing in front of us with his back to the dancehall audience. It was a few minutes before we were to start playing. Some of the musicians chuckled, apparently not concerned about his remarks. It was 1956. This was my first "name band" gig, and on a national tour.

"What did Tex mean by that?" I said, wide-eyed and innocent, leaning over to Sante Russo, the veteran saxophonist sitting beside me. Sante always seemed to know what was going on.

"You'll find out," he said with a wry smile. We searched through our music folders and pulled out the arrangements for the first set.

What was that all about? Why all the mystery? Be ready for what? Because I was new with the band, I didn't ask any more questions.

Just the usual 1956 Saturday night in Longview, Texas, I guess. And I was the lead alto saxophone player with the famous Tex Beneke Orchestra. We were on a spring-summer tour of one-nighters throughout the Midwest and South.

Bandleaders like Beneke, who had built famous reputations during the Swing Era's halcyon days, were now touring more and more to "Flyspeck, U.S.A.," performing live for pockets of fans who knew them from so many hit recordings. Since Tex had taken over the Glenn Miller Band at the end of World War II, his music library had many memorable hits, like "In The Mood," "Tuxedo Junction," "Moonlight Serenade," "String of Pearls," "Little Brown Jug," "Kalamazoo," "Serenade In Blue." And here I was, playing in his band.

I was proud to be in the band, but I did have mixed emotions again. I was excited and thrilled to be there, of course. Yet I wanted the experience to be worth the decision I had made to leave my family for another tour. I was happy, sad, anxious, hungry to learn, afraid to fail, and all too well aware this was a chance to validate myself as a professional musician, an opportunity I couldn't afford to waste.

Longview, Texas was a busy little town of ranches, farms and a few oil rigs. Post-war urban expansion and commercial development was on its way but hadn't yet taken hold. Neither had the interstate highway system. The railroad, however, ran through town. With a population of about 25,000, and 120 miles east of Dallas, it was still a cowboy town in spirit. You could see cattle being driven by cowpokes on horseback near town, crossing a road here and there to get to the railroad yard.

People generally minded their own business and worked hard in Longview. And, as I would soon discover, they played hard too, especially in their dance hall.

The Beneke band was booked to play for one night at Longview's Longhorn Ranch Dance Hall. It wasn't a ranch, and it wasn't exactly a hall but rather an almost-a-building structure, half the size of a football field, mostly open-sided, situated on a scruffy prairie about five miles from town. The Longhorn's wooden bandstand, a two-foot-high, tiered platform, sat on the concrete floor at one end of the hall. Obviously, the night air probably cooled the place. But when there was no breeze, whew!

We arrived at Longhorn Ranch on our chartered Greyhound bus at 5:00 p.m. that afternoon in June, after an eight-hour, bumpy, 300-mile haul from Tulsa. The sun was still overhead. The driver maneuvered the bus up behind the building, close to the bandstand back entrance. Once we left our air-conditioned bus and stepped outside, the first thing that hit me was the strangling heat reaching from the ground, stored up with a full day's download of Texas sun. Every time I took a deep breath I could feel the heat pouring into me. It was hot— Texas hot, June hot, Saturday night hot, sticky hot, Jack Daniels hot.

Miles of parched land stretched off into the distance, dotted with shrubs that were probably tumbleweeds in the making. I wondered why anyone would want to live out here in this dismal dirtscape.

Since we weren't staying in a hotel that night but would be traveling on the bus to the next town right after the gig, we didn't unload our bags; just our instruments, equipment, and the usual shaving cream, toothbrush and razor.

The typical one-nighter bus tour pattern was: travel all day, get to the dancehall, set up, get dressed, play the gig, get back on the bus, travel all night, arrive at the next town early in the morning and check in to a hotel, sleep till late afternoon, set up, play the gig, go back to the hotel, sleep there that night, get up the next morning, get back on the bus and start the process all over again. I adapted to the routine easily. Booking into hotels every other day and spending alternate nights traveling saved money, always a plus because band members paid for their own hotel rooms.

After setting up the music stands, lights, wires, and unpacking the music that day, Eddie Matthews, who rode with us on the bus wherever we traveled, went about the business of checking the PA system. Eddie took out Tex's gold-plated microphone to begin the sound check and connected it to a cable already in place. He did the same with the girl singer's mike. A few of us stood around to watch and listen.

"Testing, testing, one, two, three. Check, check. One, two," Eddie said. "Check, check, testing, testing …" etcetera, etcetera. Boring.

I wondered why, just for once, someone didn't say something different during a sound check. Like maybe throw in some Shakespeare, just for laughs.

> *Is this a dagger I see before me?*
> *the handle toward my hand?*
> Testing.
> *Come, let me clutch thee.*
> One, two, three.
> *I have thee not, yet I see thee still.*

Check.

Why not?

The younger musicians in the band all agreed the place sounded like a barn. Hell, it was a barn. I wanted it to sound like Carnegie Hall and expected that it should. But the musicians who had played here in past years were indifferent. They had more important things on their minds, like finding a pay phone, reading newspapers, catching up on stock market quotes, writing music, practicing, and sniffing out the locals.

Two of them already had their eyes on a couple of young women who had gathered around to watch the band set up. After all, this was a name band, a sufficient flame for some of the local moths.

The scene reminded me to call my wife, which I did every other night. The separation was rough on the family. I ran up a hellava phone bill on that tour.

The musicians felt pretty gritty after the long, hot ride. There were no showers, so after set-up we used the sinks in the men's room to wash and shave.

"Hey, guys," I said, "there's no hot water."

"Welcome to the road, man," one drawled, as he cruised his electric shaver across his face.

"What was Tex talking about when he said to be ready?" I asked Sante.

"You'll know soon enough."

"Come on, man. What's up? We going to have to march or something?"

"In a manner of speaking, yes," he said.

I really didn't get it. But I didn't want to appear too curious. I shrugged it off. We ate boxed sandwiches and had cold beers and soft drinks before going back onto the bus, which was air-conditioned, thank God. We changed into our uniforms: black tux pants, black patent leather shoes, powder blue dinner jackets with shawl collars, blue cummerbunds, white shirts and matching blue bow ties. Tex wore a midnight blue tux. This was Saturday night in Texas and Tex was a favorite son, so it was dress-up night.

We strolled onto the stand fifteen minutes early to get ready for the first set. I noticed a few ceiling fans sparsely spaced overhead, whirling around lazily, not pushing much air. Two floor fans, set up at the sides of the bandstand, aimed at us. If they were supposed to keep us cool, somebody was a dreamer, or a salesman.

Finally we were set up, tuned up and ready to go. It was eight o'clock. But just before we started, a chicken wire curtain the width of the bandstand was unfurled, lowered from the rafters in front of the stage, and secured to small hooks in the concrete floor, the bottom angling out a few feet onto the dance floor. It was like we were caged animals for everyone to look at. It turned out to be the other way around.

"Really, Sante," I said, "that's wild. I never saw that before. What's the chicken wire for?"

"You'll find out," he said, busy making adjustments to his octave key with a tiny screwdriver. Sante was a man of few words. As usual, our first tune would be Tex's signature theme song, "Moonlight Serenade," probably the most recognizable Big Band theme song of the era. It had been Glen Miller's theme, the first and last tune we played every night.

The band drew a big turnout. After all, it was Saturday night in Longview. The famous Tex Beneke Orchestra had come to town to play all the Glenn Miller hits. No self-respecting citizen could stay away, even the mayor. He introduced us with a big "Ladies and Gentlemen, as your mayor it is my distinct pleasure to present the pride of Texas, Mr. Tex Beneke himself, and his fabulous orchestra!" The crowd cheered like the freshmen bleacher section at a college football game.

"Wow," I said, "this is really something, huh, Sante? Listen to them. They love us already."

"Yeah, sure," said Sante, nodding casually.

Women looked festive in party dresses; men wore chinos, shirts and cowboy boots, some in jeans with short sleeve shirts. Others donned fancy western garb with string ties. Most kept their cowboy hats on. Some wore jackets and regular ties.

Everyone had brought liquor, and everywhere coolers were stashed full of beer. Long wooden tables with pipe legs lined both sides of the hall, facing in toward the huge dance floor like out-of-bounds markers. Each table, covered with a shiny white paper tablecloth, sported a plastic bucket of ice.

When it was "Moonlight Serenade" time, well over three thousand good citizens of Longview invaded the dance. No one was shy. No one waited for someone else to go first. They swept *en masse* out onto the concrete like a flood and immediately began dancing. After all, that's why they had come, so why waste time.

The sparkling overhead mirror ball began its slow, glittery rotations right away. No waiting to be introduced as a special effect at some appropriately romantic moment later. Hell, no. Shoot the works right away. The crowd was warmed up and raring to go. The night had started at an energy level usually not reached before the halfway point.

By nine o'clock the place was rocking like New Year's Eve at an Elks Club in Erie. The din became a roar and kept climbing. The booze was flowing. The Good Times were rolling. And boy was it hot.

After the first forty-minute set, we took a twenty-minute break. Off came our jackets. We were all sweating so much that I wondered if the crowd could smell us. I also noticed that Duke, the drummer, was missing, and so was Miss Pastel Dress Texasette Number Two, with whom he'd been chatting earlier.

Fortunately, just about then Tex called the musicians back onto the bandstand to start the next set, and the big galoots who had been approaching the band walked off. I was on stage first, ready to go, since I had a solo coming up and was silently woodshedding the notes on my horn. Duke came hustling in through the back door and ran up onto the bandstand, pushing back his hair. Oddly enough, he didn't have his shoes on. Not the best thing for a drummer, I thought. But, hey, what did I know. Anyway, he just made it behind his drums as Tex counted off.

We opened the set with one of Miller/Beneke's biggest hits, practically a household name, "Chattanooga Choo Choo." The crowd loved it and cheered as we began. The dance floor swarmed once again with eager, sweaty flesh.

After the eight-bar intro, complete with train whistle effect, and the initial sax section first chorus, Tex began singing the tune's memorable lyric, just as he had on the original Miller recording, with his distinctive throaty, nasal style and wide vibrato. Compared to singers like Sinatra, he had the romantic appeal of a lumberjack singing "Tenderly" while sawing down a Redwood. But he was truly one of the vocal originals of the big band era, and the crowd loved him.

Pardon me, Boy, is that the Chattanooga Choo Choo?
Track 29. Well you can give me a shine.

The dancers sang right along with him. It was a fun tune with an infectious beat. During Eddie Zandy's trumpet solo I noticed that both the local lovelies I'd seen earlier flirting with the band, looking like dolls, were dancing with their too-tall Texans, all smiles, probably sweet-talking their men. But all the while they were looking past them, over to the band, making eyes at their two musician dandies, who, noticing they were being noticed, began playing with an extra bit of showmanship. There's nothing like the attention of admirers to make you feel appreciated and want to perform with extra spark.

The next tune was "Skylark," a beautiful ballad by Hoagy Carmichael, composer of "Stardust." It had a challenging solo that really showed off the alto sax... and me. I loved playing it and played it well. Nobody cheered when I finished, but a quiet "That was nice," came from Sante when I sat down again. Thanks, Sante.

Six more tunes followed. By the time we got to the set-closer, "American Patrol," the crowd was practically levitating. In a whoop-it-up party mood, fueled by alcohol and by just plain pent-up energy, they demonstrated an aspect of group dynamics I hadn't observed before.

We had just finished "Patrol" when the fight broke out. And what a fight it was.

CRASH. SMASH. BAM. WHACK. Yelling. Fists connecting. Bodies colliding. Everyone seemed to be involved. It was a mass melee. But I swear some people were laughing.

When the first bottle hit the chicken wire in front of us with a sudden *wangggg*, it scared the hell out of me. I was sitting, right in the middle of the front row. More bottles followed. *Wangggg, wangggg* – empties, I surmise, judging from the state of the crowd, though the thought didn't occur to me at the time, I was too busy trying to duck. We were caught in the middle of a good ole Texas Saturday-night brawl.

"This is it, huh, Sante," I said. "This is what Tex meant?"

"You got it, man."

Each bottle that hurtled toward us bounced harmlessly onto the slack chicken wire screen, before rolling down and clanking onto the concrete.

"That's it, guys," Tex said calmly. "Pack it up."

I froze, open-mouthed. I thought for sure we might be killed. Maybe the crowd would charge the bandstand. I clutched my beautiful Selmer Alto close to me and ducked. But Tex was cool and matter-of-fact, as if it were a rehearsal. We had played only half the time for which we had been contracted, since the dance was supposed to go till midnight. But the old-timers on the band were already grabbing their horns and music and beating it out the back door onto the bus—which, I discovered, was warmed up, cooled down, and ready to roll.

Most nights it took us about an hour to strike the set, putting away horns and equipment, hanging around and loading up the bus. And that was if we were in a hurry to get on the road to make it to the next town, check in, and get some sleep. Musicians don't move too fast after playing a gig. They like to mill around and unwind.

On this night it couldn't have been more than fifteen minutes before we were out of there. All the while, the brawl continued inside with merry abandon. We changed out of our tuxes on the bus. No one seemed to be too upset, but I was shaking my head in disbelief. A crazy scene. So this is the road.

That's when Sante told me this happens every year the band plays in Longview.

"You're kidding," I said. "Then why does Tex play here?"

"Because every year they offer him more money to come back. And they always pay in advance. It's the best-paying date on the tour. And we never have to play more than half the gig before the fight starts."

Meanwhile, back at the bus...

"Jeezus, let's get out of here," said Zandy, who had been with the band for over five years. He wasn't known for risk-taking. The guys respected him. I guess he didn't want his embouchure adjusted by some crazy cowboys either.

Eddie Matthews spoke up. "You girls gotta get off now. I mean you have to leave the bus right now. We gotta go, and you can't come. Come on now, girls. Out! Now!"

With that the driver swung the door open. The girls gave the dandies long sloppy, liquor-soaked, lipstick-smeared smooches. Uck.

"Hurry up, for crissakes," Eddie said.

Two big guys in Stetsons, who had been looking *down* into the windows and pounding on the glass, were making their way around the front of the bus toward the door.

"Come on girls," Eddie yelled. "Out. Now!"

Calling out, "Bye, fellas," the two femme fatales alighted, apparently unfazed, then faced their awaiting cowboys.

"Now Hank, honey," the one named Laurie said. "We was just havin' some fun, some harmless fun. So doncha' go gettin' yourself all upset now."

Seymour slammed the door shut and gunned the motor a few times, just to let everyone know we were leaving. The two "trees" were shaking serious fists toward where they figured Duke and Nick were sitting. The girls clung to their guys' arms, doing their we-got-to-soothe-our-stupid-but-necessary-men tap dance. It appeared they knew the steps well.

The time had come to *move*. As we drove off in a cloud of Texas dust, Frank Huggins, the carefree lead trumpet player, yelled, "Hi-Ho, Silver! Away!"

I was a slim 130 pounds at the time, and five foot seven. I climbed up into the shallow overhead luggage rack, flattened a small pillow, stretched out on my back, and settled in for the all-night drive to wherever. Studying the ceiling, inches away from my nose, I asked myself if this was the glamorous career I imagined traveling on the road would be, making memorable music with a famous name band.

I listened to Duke and Nick compare notes and to Frank read aloud, laughing with sheer enjoyment at *Downbeat's* penchant for hyperbolic descriptions of idolized jazz musicians. I could overhear Eddie working his *I'm-really-an-important-guy* routine on the girl singer. Random jokes from the poker game filtered up to me as the bus lurched down the highway into the night.

How lucky I was to have made it. I was playing with a name band. Finally. But though I appreciated the opportunity immensely, something was missing. I figured this was not the way to fame and fortune, and certainly not the way I wanted to spend my life, especially with a family. The road leads nowhere. Sooner or later you're right back where you started. I would have to think carefully before touring again.

I got a little sentimental about this journey as my thoughts played a soul-searching tune about the road, returning home, and where the future might find me next.

The Father of Invention

Richard F. Hurst

Richard Hurst is my husband. My love and admiration for him will show clearly in the ponderings below. He did not think it appropriate to be part of my book. And yet, several of the men who were asked to write were most anxious to see what Richard would contribute, naturally assuming that he would. My husband is an inventor, and a successful one. He owns several patents; he knows the process from idea to design to prototype to market. And he realizes the joys of creating for a living. It is also encouraging to know that college is not for everyone. Corporate and university and government politics aren't either. Richard is not like the other guys, but fits in with everyone. He stands alone, part of his great appeal to me. Here's a refreshing glimpse at how a modern inventor with old standards makes it in today's new world. With his patent approval, I write about him here.

If necessity is the mother of invention, what is the father of invention? Perhaps it is a sense of wonder. Coupled with necessity, the two light the creative sparks from which invention is forged. And their offspring form a continuum of newness on a cosmic scale. For men, it is often the need to build, to improve; to know how something works or to make it work more efficiently, i.e. to build a better mousetrap. The desire to get from point A to point B is a factor. So is the need to advance: as an individual, as a people, and as a universe. To coin Buzz Lightyear, invention reaches to infinity and beyond.

Richard discusses these things with me as we are driving from our home in the Blue Ridge Mountains of North Carolina to our place by the sea in Vero Beach, Florida. Between those landscapes lies all possibility, which somehow makes the conversation flow more easily. Or perhaps it's just six hundred miles to cover and the opportunity to make that road time go a little bit faster.

He begins by describing two types of invention: practical and artistic. Practical invention requires three steps, the first of which is the concept or idea, followed by experimentation and application. If there is no history of something, the practice of it is experimentation. Commercial usually means practical. It is a response to a need for application. It fills a hole. The artistic is often based in more purity of form, as it is making something for the sake of it. Science introduces the *wow factor* into everyday existence. Art begs the question of wonder. Thus, invention can be a response to a perceived need or purely creative.

While Richard has written music and dabbled in painting and sculpture — and has shown some talent for it — none of his pursuits of whimsy have been commercially successful on a grand scale. And yet, to him they are just as meaningful. Pure invention — songs, poems, sculptures, paintings — is non-utilitarian. Though others find success here, there has been no major money in it for Richard. This is invention simply for sharing in the joy of creation. (I am reminded of the happiness between mother and son as her little boy proudly brings her a picture or clay model or sailboat he has made. But I keep the thought to myself.)

Everyone, he stresses, is an inventor to one degree or another, designing and implementing custom-made practicality for one's own life. It is a way to add beauty and grace to our existence; to escape the drab, the mundane, and the numbness that can set in otherwise. Richard offers these equations:

$$Interest + Enthusiasm + Hopefulness = Refreshment$$
$$and$$
$$Refreshment = Newness$$

Our talk drifts into the Zen of creating machines, a large part of the commercially successful inventions Richard designs and builds for major pharmaceutical companies. He has always had the ability to "become the machine." He can see how it will work, feel what will happen if it is designed a certain way, and know what to do to make it function smoothly. His machines are works of art and, the few times I have attended trade shows with him, I can spot a Hurst machine a mile away. They have a clean, white beauty and they are more mechanical than electronic, with a combined strength and smoothness that is a sight to behold. They are simple. They work. But no one has ever thought to do it before. They are unique in all the world.

Invention can also be hugely entertaining and just plain fun. And here we get into the physical plane rather than the intellectual or mystical, because everyone knows laughter is the best medicine. One Halloween night, Richard is home on Steeplechase Road in Devon, Pennsylvania, with son Russel who, at age twenty-eight, is struggling with liver cancer and can surely use a laugh. They have put together a machine that dispenses vials filled with rolled paper money of various denominations. The bottles' contents are hidden by shrouds, but each ghost or goblin who arrives is encouraged to choose a bottle from the tray, insert it into the machine, push the button, and wait for his or her prize. The machine *ka-chings, boings, pffffts,* belches and *zings,* in the process removing the shroud, and out pops the treat. No one knows there's a man behind the machine, or that every bottle is a good one, containing at least a dollar and at most a twenty. The happiest of all is Russel, riddled with a disease he will not survive, laughing and watching the magic, relishing in the reprieve from his real nightmare: the Grim Reaper. He munches a Snickers bar and—for once—forgets everything but the charge he gets out of seeing this Halloween Machine come to life for every kid who comes to their door.

"In order to invent," Richard continues, "you need to exclude the old to create something new, unencumbered by the past." How? First, make sure no one else has done it. Do a patent search. This is the study and investigation stage. Next, play without a computer. Make drawings that embody thoughts. Record what is plausible as you go along. It's really systematic. Finally, believe that you can do it. A huge part of the Eureka(!) moment is not requiring the support of others (who inevitably think you are crazy until you actually do it). This is impossible for people who only see what already exists. Being obligated or reliant (as when you are designing for money) does affect the purity of the process but does not negate the process that is followed. It just makes it tougher. This method has worked not only for pharmaceutical industry applications, but in his development of patented office equipment, micro-filtration, and a powdering device for the veterinary industry as well.

In 1972, Richard Hurst had an idea for what has become his most successful machine: the Hurst Label Stripper, which removes labels from vials, syringes and pharmaceutical bottles. Going to the best patent attorneys in Philadelphia, they listened, demanded $10,000 down to start, and emphasized that the fee was only the beginning. Richard didn't have $10,000. He wouldn't give up. He felt he had something.

Marshall Dann was the head of the Patents and Trademarks office in Alexandria, Virginia. Richard drove down and begged the Commissioner to hear him out and offer some advice. Mr. Dann instructed his secretary, a huge African-American woman, described in the telling as "an angel," to provide all the books he would need from their extensive library in order to learn about patent law and file his own case. In the months that followed, Richard successfully filed for, and was issued, the patent. At the completion of the process, he received a congratulatory letter from Marshall Dann of the U.S. Patent Office. (Commissioner Dann also immediately guessed the name of the big-shot patent firm in Philadelphia so eager to take a young man's money along with his bright idea.)

Another key player in this inventor's success was Joe Keating, who lived on the next farm from Richard's in Pennsylvania. He knew a senior patent attorney in Paoli for Burroughs Corporation whose son had committed suicide. Joe was trying to find some outside work with a young inventor for the attorney in order to get his mind off his tragedy. Richard jumped at the chance. This turned into an opportunity to work with a great patent attorney who never charged him a dime (but often told him over the years, "You owe me a lot of money!"). His relationship with John Sowell continues to this day. As a result, Richard has helped hundreds of others in need of experienced patent advice, at no cost. *Pro bono. Paying it forward. What goes around comes around.* There are all kinds of fancy terms for a service that was simply a duty, a responsibility and a matter of honor to him.

The label stripper patent has returned millions of dollars over a thirty-eight year period. It has been licensed to several manufacturers. It has been sold to numerous biological and pharma companies and their subsidiaries, including Amgen, Bayer, Pfizer, Genentech, G.E. Healthcare, Wyeth, and Merck. And yet, the management of Hurst Corporation, unbeknownst to its illustrious customers, has always been a one-man show. This offers all the control and reaps all the rewards, but it also demands sound judgment and wearing all the hats. Hurst has, of course, worked with advertisers, outside shops and manufacturers; but the management of the company has been his alone.

Richard is, by self-definition, a Kitchen Inventor. So, not only did he design, develop, and build the machines; he also communicated with vendors, sold the machines, assembled them, packed them up for shipment, delivered and installed. Rarely (because the need for repair is almost unheard of and often a simple vendor engineering error), he flew out to some plant and performed the required maintenance. And this he has always been happy to do.

The Hurst Label Stripper has also taken him to places all over the globe, with business trips to the United Arab Emirates, Japan, England, Ireland, Wales, Puerto Rico, Belgium, and Canada. He has eaten with paupers in Northern Ireland pubs and been the guest of sheikhs in the U.A.E. He has ice-fished in minus-25 degree temperatures in Winnipeg and felt the blast of 125-plus-degrees heat in the deserts of Ras Al Khaimah. Workers applauded in Marietta, Pa., when presented with a demonstrated mechanical device that would save hours of time and ensure on-the-job safety. A machine operator in Italy once kissed the hands of the *presidente* for providing his means of work and livelihood at Fiat Pharmaceuticals. They did not speak the same language, but the worker most certainly conveyed his message.

These many experiences dispel the myth of the Inventor as Mad Scientist, surrounded by bubbling cauldrons and steaming beakers in some secluded lab. Richard has always known how to talk with people, to listen with his heart, to know instinctively what they need, and to tell a good story. He understands that good manners are really a way of putting those around you at ease. He is comfortable with all strata of the social spectrum and has proven himself to be a citizen of the world. Being an inventor, he has always known that you have to leave everything behind when you travel to a new place. In this way, you are unlimited by things previously seen, and can jump in with both feet.

Like a river, invention is continually emptying yourself so that a new stream can flow. Stagnant water is nowhere, and it's boring. For the inventor, the babbling brook, the ocean wave, the waterfall, the spring creek so full to bursting it washes over the road, have always held more appeal. Conceiving an idea and bringing it to fruition is the wellspring of joy.

In the end, his advice is that if you really want to do something, the only thing holding you back is yourself. Money is not the only measure of success, but it is, of course, the practical one. Still, inspiration and desire can add beauty to even the most practical invention. And lo, even though only a few of his patents have been commercially successful, they are all valuable because they express something heretofore unknown, pleasing for a myriad of reasons. Each encompasses the urgency of necessity and the excitement of wonder in discovering the new.

To Richard F. Hurst, inventing is sharing a deep spiritual plane with one's God. Invention takes us to that higher place, beyond the confines of self, into the realm of creation.

Man Overboard
A story from the decks of a U.S. Navy ship
Robert Jackson

This may sound a little strange, but I was once Robert's boss. In keeping with modern times, I actually met Robert when he came to work under my supervision at the Michigan Department of Corrections. He had been a Corrections Officer, injured on the job, and basically reassigned to a desk job in Central Office. I was the Procurement and Contracts Manager for the department, and Robert was given the job of Forms Control, literally to keep track of and dispense the thousands of forms created and used throughout the prison administrative system. Robert is a bulldog outside and an old softie inside. His pets, shared with wife Ann Marie, have always been bulldogs. A favorite of mine was Vinnie, a gentle dog taken to a veterinary farm when he became ill. When the Jacksons returned to pick up their pet, they were told Vinnie didn't make it. Something didn't smell right, and Robert set up a sting operation where he sent a friend out to the farm in an attempt to purchase his dog back. There sat Vinnie, healthy and ready for sale. Robert got his dog back. The tale he relates below is another mission accomplished — of the human kind.

On 14 September 1979 while berthed at U.S. Naval Station, Charleston, South Carolina, my friend J.T. (Joseph Thomas) Kelley from Quincy, Massachusetts and I were doing what we usually did onboard the *USS Compass Island*. We were sitting in the Hull Maintenance Technician (HT) Shop Office watching our three- or four-channel black and white small screen TV and complaining or arguing about whatever came to mind. Many times the discussion centered on who was going to turn the channel or who would go below decks to buy the Cokes out of the vending machine. Neither one of us could leave the ship as we both had duty. Kelley and I were the on-duty Hull Techs. In addition to running that night's emergency drill, if there was a fire on the ship we were expected to lead the firefighting team. If the ship began flooding, we were expected to stop the flooding and remove the water. In general, the HTs were the catch-all group for emergency situations.

On this particular night, Kelley and I were complaining about our Sounding and Security watches. Our four-hour watch consisted of wandering around the ship looking for existing or impending emergency situations. Every hour we were expected to report, in person, "all secure" to the Officer of the Deck (OD) on the Quarterdeck (an area of the ship designated by the Commanding Officer where official functions are carried out when the ship is in port). Of course, emergency situations were reported immediately.

Kelley had the "20 by" watch (7:45pm to 11:45pm) and I had the mid-watch (11:45 p.m. to 3:45 a.m.). I hated the mid-watch! You just get to sleep and then a flashlight shines in your face, wakes you and an unseen person tells you *Jackson, time for watch.* After the watch, by the time you shower and get to bed it is after 4 a.m. and with reveille at 6:30 a.m., the mid-watch makes for a short night. Since JT wanted to go to bed and get some sleep before watch and I hated the mid-watch, we traded watches.

I do not remember who had the 16 (4 p.m.) to 20 (8 p.m.) watch, but at 1945 the HT shop hatch opened and the 16-to-20 watch person walked into the shop looking to be relieved. We walked out to the Quarter Deck where we found the OD. The person on watch came to attention and saluted and said, "Sounding and Security Watch reports all secure and properly relieved by HT3 Jackson." I came to attention, saluted the OD and said, "Assume the watch." The OD returned our salutes.

I walked back to the HT shop and closed the hatch. Closing the hatch served two purposes; one, it kept the Charleston, South Carolina bugs out of the shop and two, served as a burglar alarm. The shop was always losing tools and when the hatch opened, anyone in the shop would look to the hatch to see who was coming in.

In the shop office Kelley was still watching TV. I reminded him about the mid-watch and he brushed away my concerns. I watched a little TV and then headed out on my first watch round. Around thirty minutes later, I reported all secure to the OD and returned to the HT shop. Kelley was still in the office watching TV. After thirty minutes I left the shop for my second watch round. When I returned to the shop, JT was still watching TV. This continued my entire watch.

At 2345 (11:45 p.m.), I asked Kelley, "You ready?" Kelley grumbled as we walked to the quarter deck and, with the same formality as four hour earlier, he assumed the Sounding and Security Watch. We both went back to the HT shop to watch TV.

When Kelley left the shop for his first watch round, I stayed behind to watch TV. When Kelley came back to the shop, I was still there. This process continued until 0345. When Kelley left to be relieved from his watch, I finally went to bed.

At 0425 the emergency alarm went off and the emergency announcements began. I jumped up and began getting dressed thinking *what can I do to save time?* The emergency announcement was repeating over and over, and said, "This is not a drill; this is not a drill, man overboard on the *USS Compass Island.*"

I skipped my socks and a t-shirt, pulling my work shoes onto my bare feet and my work shirt over my bare chest. I ran to the scene, buttoning my shirt on the way. When I got to the scene, I saw many standing around doing nothing but looking over the side of the ship at the guy, a fellow shipmate, drowning in the water. All the life rings on the ship have been tossed to this guy and he was not able to get them. I can see them floating down the river, strobe lights flashing away.

People are approaching me, telling me and asking what to do. No one was taking charge, the place was chaos and I needed help. The first thing I did was point to two guys and told them to both get battle lanterns (high powered flashlights powered by two dry cell batteries). They asked from where and I told them the repair locker or anywhere else they can find one. Next, I pointed at the Officer of the day (Officer in Charge of the ship in the Captain's absence) to act as crowd control and push people back.

I then saw Danny DeWolf from the Deck Division and my buddy JT Kelley in the front of the crowd. Danny was "Duty Deck," the Deck Division guys who are responsible for, among other things, the ship's ropes and lines. I pointed to Danny D and Kelley and told them to go to the life jacket locker and get a life jacket. Go to the rope locker and get a good long medium-sized rope and turn on the capstan (think winch) to help us pull the guy up.

The battle lantern guys returned. I told them where to stand, apart and not over the man in the water. If they dropped the light, I did not want it to land on this guy's head. I also told them to shine the lights near the man in the water, not on him, so he was not blinded.

Then Danny tells me that even though he is duty deck the lifejacket locker and the rope locker are both locked and he does not have the key. We now have no lifejacket, no rope, and no winch because the power switch was in the rope locker. Without missing a beat, I told Danny and Kelley to get me that fire hose and I pointed to the fire hose station on the aft bulkhead of repair locker three. Many people loudly questioned why get a fire hose? I do not have time to respond as I have a man in the water.

During all these processes I am yelling encouragement to the guy in the water. *Hold on, we are coming, we are on our way, stay strong.* Danny and Kelley get back with the fire hose. Someone yells take off the nozzle to which I yelled back shut up and leave it on. I told Danny to remove the slack in the hose and give anything extra to the crowd. I figured if the crowd held the hose they would really be of help instead of trying to help which was really no help at all.

I told the guys with the battle lanterns what to do. I pointed at one and yelled you keep your light on the water. He nodded he understood. I pointed at the other battle lantern guy and yelled you keep your light on the hose nozzle. His light immediately switched from the water to the nozzle.

As Kelley and I lowered the fire hose, everything either grew quiet or I became so focused I tuned it out. As the nozzle got closer to the man in the water, my heart beat faster. Finally, he had the nozzle! We dropped about five more feet of hose and people are yelling he has the nozzle, pull him up.

Danny D and Kelley were with me and ignored the crowd. I yelled to the guy in the water, let the hose slide through your hands and put the nozzle between your feet. Treading water is hard work and I did not want this guy to get halfway up (or more) to safety and lose his grip and fall back to the water. Once he did this, I told him when you feel strong enough we will pull you up.

I told the battle lantern guys, as we pull him up, put the light on his feet so we can see him and he is not blinded; both nodded acknowledgment. I asked Danny if he was ready; he was. I looked at Kelley and said something about the nap he skipped while I was on watch. He smiled so I asked if he was ready; he was. I told the crowd to only take what hose Danny fed backwards to them; do not pull. Danny nodded. A few minutes (maybe seconds) went by and the guy in the water said he was ready.

Hand over hand, Kelley and I pulled up the fire hose with our shipmate standing on the nozzle. Danny pulled out the slack in the fire hose as it hit the deck behind us and the crowd took up Danny's slack.

Despite the heavy weight, Kelley and I did not stop while we were pulling. When he got to the top, he reached up and grabbed the bulwark (the wall extending the ship's sides above the deck) and we pulled him back onto the ship.

Another mission accomplished.

USS COMPASS ISLAND (AG-153)
FPO NEW YORK O9501   IN REPLY REFER TO:

The Commanding Officer, USS COMPASS ISLAND (AG-153) takes great pleasure in expressing appreciation to:

HULL MAINTENANCE TECHNICIAN THIRD CLASS

ROBERT PAUL JACKSON

U. S. NAVY

for service as set forth in the following
CITATION:

"For outstanding performance of duty while on board USS COMPASS ISLAND (AG-153) at U. S. Naval Station, Charleston, South Carolina at about 0425, 14 September 1979. Your rapid response to a man overboard emergency resulted in a fellow shipmate being rescued from drowning. Your knowledge of rescue equipment and professionalism at the scene set a fitting and proper example for your shipmates to follow. Your actions reflect great credit upon yourself, this command, and were in keeping with the highest traditions of the United States Naval Service. Well done!

G. Q. GEIST
COMMANDER, U. S. NAVY
COMMANDING OFFICER

The Journey

Jeremy Jones

Jeremy Jones grew up in Detroit, attended Michigan State University, wants to overcome the limitations of his beginnings and take advantage of the opportunities he has sought after via education and enthusiasm. This guy is fresh out of college, all those ideas derived from his business classes are simmering in his head; he dresses for success and pursues excellence. He has what it takes to put together a team and start an online company called Advidnation. Some young entrepreneur might read this and be encouraged to improve, get started, to make something of him- or herself. My wish is that Jeremy will consider that there are moments when perfection exists in all of us, always fleeting, but there in pure form nonetheless. This wisdom comes from experience, an insight each person is free to arrive at or ignore. It is not a denial of God; rather an affirmation. Awareness makes it happen all the sooner. But, in the meantime, here's a plan for success going down in East Lansing, Michigan, by way of a confident and determined Jeremy Jones.

I started developing Advidnation in December of 2010, after having had the idea for about a year.

Prior to beginning Advidnation, I was developing a business I was much more passionate about—Pioneer Lending, a company designed to change the way the world looks at finance. I had spent a year-and-a-half developing the company, putting together a detailed business plan, and assembling a talented

Board of Advisors, when I realized that it would take longer then I liked to get the investment needed to launch the company.

At this point, I decided to turn to fundraising methods I had more control over and launched Advidnation, with the intention of funding Pioneer Lending with its profits. As it turned out, Advidnation is a much more popular concept and easier for investors and others to understand.

First, some background. Advidnation is an online company designed specifically for the user to capitalize on his or her own content. By going to advidnation.com and signing on, a person can upload videos, pictures, blogs and more. With each form of media chosen, potential is there to earn money on the content produced. The money is earned primarily by advertisements the Advid team receives and matches with selected content for best potential response. Up to fifty percent of the earnings produced by the ads (more with special promotions) goes to the content creator.

The concept is simple: We want to share the advertising money we receive off uploaded content with the user—not keep it all to ourselves like other top sites. When I say share, I mean split—the user will receive at least fifty percent of the advertising revenue earned from selected uploads.

The biggest indicator of whether or not a submission will be chosen for ad placement is the number of hits or *clicks* that content receives. Another indicator is how often a user is uploading new material. Once the individual (or group) has confirmed that an advertisement may be placed on a selected video, they will begin earning money. Each time someone new sees that content or clicks on the ad associated with it, the creator will earn money.

When I began to delve into Advidnation, the ideas just came pouring in, and it's exciting to see my ideas riding this wave. I wanted to combine the best features of social networking and self-promotion sites with a share of the profits earned to those placing the content.

I began talking with friends and building on the basic concept. I put together a team that presently includes me as founder and CEO, an executive of music relations, a VP and user representative, an executive media producer, and a marketing person. They are a mixed group of men and women of diverse races and cultures. I wanted our team to represent a broad spectrum of participants and users. We are all young, but that provides the energy I felt was required to bring this project to the forefront, and college students are our primary focus.

After many late night sessions and endless discussions, and the creation of a website and videos to explain the basics, Advidnation was launched. We've brought in contract managers, researched patents and copyrights, and hired programmers and developers to help with the technical aspects. At this moment, there is still a long journey ahead.

This is what I believe will help the team and me get through this journey, possibly offering motivation to others.

The journey to success requires a person to look at himself first and evaluate if he has what it takes to make it. To start a business and see it through demands mental stability and positive self-esteem because you will possibly fail many times, and probably embarrass yourself a few times along the way. I believe that it is important to have a basic understanding of self because it aids you in overcoming obstacles and withstanding attacks on your self-worth. There are many people who are capable of great things but, because they do not value themselves enough to believe they can achieve their dreams, they never even try. Believing you can do it is the first step of the journey.

I have learned that—whether it is life, work, creative pursuits, or a business enterprise—no one makes it through the journey alone. I believe you are only as good as those you choose to associate with for knowledge and wisdom in your day-to-day life. I heard once that a wise man is a man who chooses to be around people who are better than himself. This is why I am confident in my personal journey to success: because of the team I am privileged to be a part of. *(A good laugh now and then doesn't hurt, either!)*

In order to foster relationships with high quality people, you have to make sure that you are bringing something to help them to become better too. What do you have to offer? What do you bring to the table? There are several characteristics I have found helpful (and can be developed if lacking) in bringing together a great team.

Leadership is a key factor. I personally try to stay open and listen to what others are saying, because there is always something to learn, and usually something that can be taken away to help you grow in leadership. But the ability to assess, to make decisions, to problem solve, to take action and ensure outcomes, while bringing out the best in others, all begin with leadership.

Having vision is very important, as it is the tool that guides the journey. Vision is one thing I hold on to dearly. Vision comes from an idea, pursuing that idea, and remaining confident that the concept can be taken from dream to reality. Vision is the guiding point for action.

My strongest leadership characteristics are motivation and perseverance. I believe these are what have helped me get this far, and what will help me get through the rest of the journey. Everyone has their own motivations, and regardless of what those may be, it is important to maintain them or small obstacles could easily trip you up—small obstacles like money, illness, and setbacks in the plan, or loss of someone on the team, to name a few.

Personally, my deepest motivation is to have a purpose in life. I find quotes are a great way to find perseverance and help keep me grounded on the journey. There will always be obstacles in life, but they are only stepping stones to a great future. Success is always located on the other side of inconvenience. Martin Luther King (many speeches and inspirational quotes), William A. Ward ("Study while others are sleeping; work while others are loafing; prepare while others are playing; and dream while others are wishing"), and Stephen R. Covey *(Seven Habits of Highly Effective People)* are other influences that encourage my efforts and guide me in my endeavors.

Find some quotes that have meaning for you, tack them up or put them on Facebook, and refer to them every once in a while. They offer the right spark at the right moment and remind you of what's meaningful. A humorous quote can be just the boost needed when you're feeling a little down (eschewing booze and drugs, of course).

Naturally, there are still times when I feel lost and detached from my vision. During those times, a few simple things help me maintain focus. First is my faith. It is empowering to have a source you can go to for wisdom, guidance, and direction. *Faith is the substance of things hoped for, the evidence of things not seen* (Hebrews 11:1). Maintaining my faith has helped me trust that I will succeed, and reading the Bible has inspired me to maintain a vision beyond everyday matters.

Music has proven to be a motivating force for me as well. Certain artists have so much intensity in their music and delivery that listening makes me want to get up and do something! Friends are also important when motivation is elusive. It's good to have people around you who are rooting for you, and truly want to see you succeed.

Now that I have done all that talking about myself, I also submit that it is important to stay humble and know there are always things about you that could be better. We are all on a continuum of constant growth, maintaining, or setback. Leaving room for yourself to grow is very important because you will never be perfect. However, striving for perfection helps you achieve excellence. One of my favorite quotes, by Vince Lombardi, states: "We are to give perfection one hell of a chase, and if we never get it, we'll certainly catch excellence along the way!"

What helps me remain humble is keeping people around me who are better than I am in different areas. This sets a standard, and constantly offers a higher ground. I also choose to make sure my actions and goals also make other people's lives better. The more you share and give to others, the more you receive from them in return. My experience in business has been that many people are so focused on what they can get that they limit themselves in how much they could receive.

In the classic book, *How to Win Friends and Influence People*, Dale Carnegie stressed that what you give is what you will receive. *What goes around comes around; Karma; the Golden Rule,* each describes basically the same concept. If you raise your voice, the other person will raise his voice. You hurt someone and he will want to hurt you back. You try to limit someone; he is naturally going to want to break free.

It works that way in business, an excellent point to remember in negotiations: you give, they will give back. Sharing with others leads to the desire to share in return. Awareness of this point is a significant milestone: not only are we dependent on one another, but actions lead to reactions and people respond to our individual actions in kind. This awareness can change the way we interact dramatically, and seriously affect outcomes. There's a catch, though. Sharing and giving must come from genuine motives, or eventually they will fail. The good news is that when practiced with good intentions, this automatically becomes the norm. It just happens.

These things have helped me get to the point where I am now. I have not yet reached what I consider success, but I have shared what I believe will lead me to success. I have already accomplished a few milestones; more challenges await me. My goal in sharing my thoughts and experiences is to help and inspire you to recognize your talents, to pursue your vision and dreams, to know that you can do it, and that you don't have to be alone in the process of getting there.

As author and lecturer Gil Bailie wrote, "Don't ask yourself what the world needs. Ask yourself what makes you come alive, and go do that, because what the world needs is people who have come alive."

Improve yourself and make the whole world better!

The Banker from Boone

Charles William (Bill) Lewis

Bill Lewis is my banker and financial planner. He's also a friend. My husband and I met him in Vero Beach, Florida, island of banks and investment firms. Imagine our surprise when we bought a house in the Boone-Blowing Rock area of North Carolina and found that Bill's family has owned land in Daniel Boone country for hundreds of years. A banker through-and-through, Bill is always impeccably dressed in business suit with crisp white shirt, cufflinks, a tie, expensive leather shoes and — yes — socks, even in the tropics. But he also has the South in his soul and loves to reminisce about growing up on farm livin'. I thank him for choosing not to write about hiding the cat in the mailbox and scaring the bejeezus out of the mailman. He does mention the mailman in a very nice context. Bill has a lot of "prank" stories, all healthy, hilarious — and harmless. Bill Lewis reminds me of the old saying, "If you want to be happy, you have to be good." Or, as Santa Claus would say, "So be good for goodness' sake!" This is not to be confused with being dull or boring. Think Country Sophisticate…no, Southern Gentleman.

I grew up on the ancestral mountain farm near Boone, N.C. in a little community known as MEAT CAMP, named for Daniel Boone's actual meat camp, which was one of the places he stored his meat caches as he traveled back and forth from his home in the Yadkin Valley to Kentucky. One of the first places to be settled in Ashe County, the remnants of the original mill, and the one built by John Moretz to replace it, can still be seen down by the old mill stream. Our farm had been in the family for over a hundred years by the time I was born. Oh, if that old farm and farmhouse could talk, what stories could be told!

I was the middle of seven children, or as Mom used to say, "the pivot point," three older and three younger — four boys and three girls. We didn't have much, but did we learn valuable lessons about life, love and tenacity! I vowed I would rise above the socio-economic level in which I grew up. Not that I ever believed that any measure of wealth would make a big difference in my basic belief system, but I *did* believe that an education and good job would garner a quality of life that could not be attained otherwise.

I was with my dad, who was a well-known builder, one day when he stopped in to see his friend and banker Alfred Adams, who was the president of the bank. They knew each other well. I was seventeen years old and was so impressed with his office, and the way he was dressed, and his confidence, his manners and mannerisms. I asked him, "What does a person need to do to become a banker?" His answer was just what I expected it to be: get a good education, learn as much as you can, work hard, don't accept defeat, be sincere, don't develop bad habits; be honest, and never take yourself too seriously. You can always be replaced. In other words, have humility.

And even though my dad thought being a banker was OK, it didn't represent the work ethic he had known all his life. He said bankers didn't know much about real work like he had known on the farm and as a builder. You must shed some perspiration to be doing real work. However, it seemed to me that what the bank president did was a LOT more appealing.

So I decided that was what I wanted to be, a banker!

After taking some courses at Appalachian State, I came to Florida and Vero Beach in 1964, got a job at Piper Aircraft, and enrolled in the new banking and finance program at Indian River Junior College in Fort Pierce. After a few years of working full-time and attending classes at night, I was granted a degree. Then I learned that Florida Atlantic University was opening a facility in Fort Pierce, offering a baccalaureate curriculum in Economics, among others. I jumped at it!

I had become friendly with a fellow in one of my classes who worked at a local Savings and Loan Association in Vero Beach. He told me he thought there might be a job opening soon and told me who to see about applying. That became my first bank job. I spent the next ten years or so in various banking positions.

Then one day I was offered an opportunity with Merrill Lynch as a financial advisor, or as was called then "account executive." My dream had come true! Securities were fascinating to me and really my main area of interest. Without doubt, I was the only kid who ever grew up at Meat Camp who became a stockbroker! I went through Merrill's training program in NYC, spending eight weeks in rigorous study designed to prepare for the National Association of Securities Dealers or NASD (today known as Financial Industry Regulatory Authority or FINRA) series 7 and 63 licenses, as well as learning the business of securities. I knew for sure I was on the right path! I subsequently earned several other securities licenses which allowed me to broaden my expertise and offer a wider array of investments to my clients. And now, as I enter my first weeks of retirement, my career has spanned some forty years in the financial services business, all right here in beautiful Vero Beach, Florida; and I humbly admit that I have enjoyed considerable success both in business as well as in personal growth and development, and enjoyment of life.

Of course, there've been setbacks and disappointments, but that's where tenacity comes in. It's the old farm sense of getting back on that horse when you fall off. When you get down, get right back up and move on! You might get lucky now and then, but you sure can't count on it.

While I was moving along through my career, my daughter, who came along early in my life, grew up in Vero Beach, becoming the Valedictorian of her graduating class at Vero Beach High School. Later she graduated from Vanderbilt University and London School of Business and Economics. Today she is a writer in Atlanta, Georgia. Linda has told me many times that the best thing that has happened to her in life is my telling her of my experiences growing up in that little mountain hamlet near Boone, N.C., because all those moral and ethical principles she learned from me emanated from those early days on the farm. I do not mean to say she didn't also learn a lot from her mother, who was my high school sweetheart, and also grew up in Boone, and worked hard as I did and became a registered nurse. Our daughter has been the great joy of our lives.

It's been a very long road from the life I knew as a child. However, I view my early years with great nostalgia and still stand by those very ideals I learned growing up. I remember and reminisce a lot about the local folks like William "Will" Winebarger, who owned a grist mill and processed grains for neighboring farmers. When he sneezed from all the "chaft" in the air, he could be heard for miles! Then there were our neighbors the Norrises, who plowed and cultivated their land with the orneriest mules on earth. Arvil Miller operated a country store nearby and was known to take a nip of moonshine now and then. And there was Clyde Winebarger (don't know if he was related to Will, but he probably was somewhere along the line) who delivered mail to the rural community. His renderings of great gospel hymns could be heard as he drove along the route in his Model T.

I remember discussions of faraway exotic places at the supper table (not dinner, that was the noon meal) that sounded so romantic and exciting. We thought that when we died, we'd surely go to Winston Salem or if REALLY lucky, maybe Charlotte, which sounded so like paradise I was sure it was where heaven must be.

It all boils down to this, and my life is a good example: You can make it if you want to, but you'll also need to live by those positive values that are so vital to a successful career as well as being a good, honest, and decent human being. My life hasn't been perfect, but it's been rewarding and satisfying, with my share of laughter and happy times; a farm boy who realized his dreams of becoming a banker.

The Provider

Michael Lineberry

Michael Lineberry is my brother-in-law. I didn't even like him that much at first. He was a little rough for me and didn't seem like a sensitive kind of guy and I wasn't too sure about one of his brothers either. After he married my sister Carolyn and I got to know him a bit, I saw much more. When I married my husband Richard, he and Mike hit it off famously: two German Krauts with deep voices and subtle humor and strong hearts, married to two Boyce sisters (Oh, lord…). I also started noticing how much he did around the house. All the manly things, like fixing and mowing and putting up Christmas lights. But other things too, like cooking and coaching and hunting and fishing. Also fun to go out and have dinner and a few drinks with. At my grandfather's funeral, the priest said, "Never underestimate the strength of a quiet man." I think that holds true for Mike. And I hope he lives a long time and enjoys the hunt to the finish, because now I love the guy. What follows is a collaboration between the two of us.

There is something ancient and true about the man who is a provider. In prehistoric times — meaning before recorded history, not that we don't know anything about them — the men were hunters and the women were gatherers. Even as clans wandered from place to place with the seasons, and after they began to settle in farms and villages. Hunting meant food, clothing, warmth, shelter, protection, life. Evidence supports the fact that men hunted and made fires and drew pictures on cave walls for centuries while women learned edible plants and herbal cures, made clothing from animal skins, wove baskets from grasses and reeds, and tended the babies. It remained the pattern until modern times when technological, social, and cultural change allowed men and women to take on a variety of roles.

Michael Lineberry is no caveman, but he is the quintessential provider. He is trained as a finish carpenter and has always managed to find work despite the horrendous economy of Michigan. A union trade, he worked his way into management and has supervised the construction of new hospital wings, retail establishments and other commercial and community buildings. His blond, blue-eyed wife teaches mostly Arab students at a school in Dearborn, Michigan. Living in Canton, a suburb of Detroit located northwest of the metropolitan airport, together they have been able to purchase a home, see sporting and cultural events, shop at high-end malls, and send their son and daughter to good schools.

Michael is a fisherman and a deer hunter. He likes to cook what he provides and I can personally attest to his grilled salmon, biscuits and gravy, pork loin with apples and cinnamon, and the holiday turkey roasted to perfection. As with most men of a certain age, his waist is expanding and his weight fluctuates, depending on how hard he tries. But Mike enjoys good food and a stiff drink, a reflection of the fruits of his labors.

In this not uncommon picture of life in the suburbs, there's other fun to be had. For years his parents (just Mom now, since his dad passed away) have had a place on Bear Lake, a short distance from Lake Michigan; and he has always relished time in the ramshackle place, surrounded by vast fields, a stone pit perfect for campfires and ghost stories, and a short hike downhill to the water. At home in Canton, the lawn is always mowed, flowers planted, the bushes trimmed. There are barbecues in summer. Christmas lights go up Thanksgiving week-end and come down by New Year's, the times when everyone has a shared break before returning to work and school.

On a lovely November day in sunny Florida, Mike's wife, Carolyn, visits with us while he and son Brad are deer hunting in the woods of Northern Michigan. Carolyn has a new iPhone, and the addiction to check, text, and record everything constantly has already set in. She is sending them video shorts of our boat ride down the Intracoastal Waterway in Vero Beach. Manatees lumber slowly down the canals and raise their heads occasionally to breathe. The fish are jumping. We speed up the boat and dolphin frolic in its wake. A baby blue heron or snowy white egret takes flight.

Meanwhile, Brad is returning photos from his environs while his dad loads up the truck. A picture comes through of a five-point deer Brad has shot that very day. Mike has bagged a couple too, and the carcasses lie in the bed of the truck, limp and lifeless. Carolyn doesn't really want to see this, but also knows they will soon be off to the place that processes the deer into meat for the table. She is far from a pioneer woman, but admits to enjoying Mike's venison stew.

Growing up the oldest of four brothers and choosing a trade that demands precise application and skilled workmanship, it was a fair prediction that Mike would be independent, organized and disciplined—and he is. Finishing what you start is a personal credo. These traits have been passed on to son Brad and daughter Nicki, a high school student who has studied dance since the age of five, but especially to Brad.

Mike played baseball as a kid and, like many fathers, hopes to realize his failed dreams of pro ball in his son. Since Brad was five and first signed up for T-ball, he has loved the game of baseball, and Mike has been there to coach him, offer advice, and help guide a boy with a natural talent and instinctive method of play, good enough to earn a college baseball scholarship. Eschewing offers from Big Ten universities, Brad wisely chooses a local school that promises lots of field play, individual attention and a chance to shine. The team travels and Mike gets a taste of several different cities, particularly drawn to Phoenix, Arizona. He can easily talk about stats for his Detroit home teams—the Lions, Tigers, Pistons and Red Wings—but his loyalties clearly lie with the Madonna Crusaders.

A career in the minors or the major leagues is not out of the question for Brad. This is the stuff dreams are made of, but in the end they are the dreams of the son unfulfilled by the father. Michael does have the satisfaction of knowing he has fulfilled the role of the ancient hunter in the modern primary provider: of food, shelter, clothing, dance costumes, sports equipment, uniforms, tuition, and travel expenses for his family. There is also the contentment to be had when the student surpasses the master. For him, this is the major indicator of a job well done.

Mike's German ancestry adds gruffness and strength to his Bavarian personality, hiding the teddy bear he really is. Approaching retirement with the cubs increasingly on their own, he is already realizing the pain of the empty cave. He knows it's natural for them to be with friends, a boyfriend or girlfriend, but complains that the awareness doesn't make it any easier for dear ol' dad. As he ages, the natural progression cannot help but push him forward into the next phase of whatever is in store. His wife is younger, with years to go until retirement, and the added worry of whether or not a school pension will still be there for

her when she does. But both hear compliments about the
capabilities and the manners of their children, and are reassured
of doing *something* right.

And the father considers another primary mission of the
Provider accomplished: to reproduce. Finally, Michael Lineberry
can take a look back over what he has done in the past without
regret, enjoy the present as it unfolds, and rest assured of hope
for the future. He nods off and sees himself with Carolyn in a
nice house in Arizona…a stadium with All-Star Brad Lineberry
on the field. Then Nicolette in a dance company, with her name
up in lights. Or maybe a teacher, like her mother.
Grandchildren…the clan continues!

The Illustrated Man

Gary Michaels

As soon as you meet Gary Michaels you can tell he's a self-made man. A strange mix of uncertainty (because he's not mainstream) and cocky (because he knows how to make things happen), Gary is a retro kind of guy who's always ready with the next new idea. For these reasons, he was successful at a very young age, and has continually become engaged in different projects and careers. The one point of great stability for Gary appears to be his daughter, Robin. They have gone through much of life together, and she has always been a bright spot in his somewhat unsettled existence. Now she's married, has two daughters of her own, and just passed the Florida bar exam. Her dad couldn't be prouder. Gary got his early start in New York but ended up in Miami. Here's the story, in his own words, of a poster business and other crazy schemes that happened to work, and the experiences that brought this man to where he is today.

I was born on a mountain top in Tennessee. No wait, that's Davey Crockett's story.

Mine begins in the Bronx in February 1943 when I was born to Rose Rosenthal Miranda. My mother had rheumatic fever when she was younger and her heart was damaged and weak, to the point where doctors advised her never to become pregnant.

She didn't want to live if she couldn't have a child. I am that child and no child had a better, more devoted, proud and loving mother.

We lived with my grandparents in a walk-in apartment at the corner of Macombs and Inwood. My mother always worked outside the home, as did my grandfather, so I was home with my grandmother. She called me *mein kind* (my child), and I understood Yiddish before I could speak English.

Our house (everyone in New York called their apartment their "house") was the center of our family. My mother had four siblings who added eleven grandchildren to the family mix, including myself. This loving household was also the scene of some conflict between my mother and her parents, and the usual arguments and psychodrama that ensue when a large, Jewish, New York family gets together in one place.

I mention my mother especially because she made me the man I am today. She worked as a hatcheck girl in some of NYC's finest hotels and restaurants. In addition to life, she gave me good genes, appreciation for music and the written word, and more love than any child could dream of. She also gave me good moral values, a sense of ethics, compassion for others, the importance of charity, and a taste for the finer things in life. Mom brought me along to parties and fine dinners where she was working the hatcheck counter. Theatre friends set up folding chairs at the end of the third row so we could see shows for free. An unforgettable afternoon was spent seeing Barbra Streisand in her first Broadway appearance.

When my mother became an office manager for a commercial factoring company, she asked me to meet her at Whitehouse and Hardy one day when I was eighteen years old. I was shuffled upstairs to the custom department and fitted for a bespoke suit. Can you imagine? This boy from the Bronx with a tailor-made suit, outfitted as if he were a king.

This may seem off-track, but my grandfather had a hand in making me the man I am, too, and his story shapes mine. Escaping Russia just ahead of the Cossacks with cunning, guts and fortitude, Grandfather made his way to England where he met my grandmother and fell in love. Here's the kicker. He had no money. She had enough saved to book one overseas passage to America. They both wanted to go to the United States, *where all things are possible and the streets are paved with gold.* In an act of blind faith, she bought his passage and he said he would send for her. My grandfather arrived in New York and found work pulling a cart (it was cheaper to pay him two dollars a week than to feed a horse). One day, after twelve hours of back-breaking work, he treated himself to a Turkish bath and massage. The masseur had a mayonnaise jar full of cash, tips earned that day. Grandpa was amazed. His friend the masseuse told him, "Aaron, you should come to work here and be a masseur." That was the end of pulling a cart and the beginning of a new life.

Aaron did become a masseur. He saved his money. He sent for Grandma and was devoted to her his entire life. His work as a masseur led him to found the Russian Rubbers Union (as in *rub down* not *prophylactics*). He never changed careers again and served as president of the Union — without compensation — for thirty-five years. My grandfather took me to the Turkish Baths and to union meetings when I was a boy. By his actions and example, I learned that I could accomplish anything I wanted as long as I worked hard and stayed the course. These lessons have served me well.

I am not the kind of guy who knew from the time he was young where he was headed. I've had tons of different jobs because I wanted to earn my own way, never stayed long in something I didn't really like, and believe that life is meant to hold a variety of experiences. During the early years I worked many jobs, from selling coffee and peanuts to measuring tuxedos for a wedding planning company. I married in May 1968, and in August 1969 my daughter, Robin, was born. I ended up raising Robin and she traveled everywhere with me. The love of a father for his daughter is profound, and today we remain close. She has brought incredible joy to my life.

The late sixties and early seventies were a great time to be young and living in New York City. Pop music could be heard at Fillmore East and other hot spots. Dancing was all the rage at places like Sybil Burton's (Richard's ex) Arthur Discotheque, where period icons Tennessee Williams, Princess Margaret, Lee Remick, Nureyev, and Truman Capote were all regulars. Young people dressed with flair, and partied, and cared about peace and Power to the People. I felt I could be successful at anything I tried and was ready to try something new.

Opportunity knocked while having dinner with my brother-in-law one night. He had been a salesman for Mattel toys and left them to work for a small poster company. Posters were used as art, to make a statement, to post the circus or a play, to cover the walls of college student dorms, but they were also a status symbol for celebrities, particularly in the music industry. He invited me to join him in starting our own company, and I agreed. My partner and I were long-haired and had a rebellious edge but were never hippies. The two of us were flat-out businessmen with a creative side, moving into what we thought was a strong and growing market. The margins were there. We knew about packaging, advertising, display, point of sale and how to stretch a dollar. Our idea was to bring posters to everyone, make them easily available, and print with quality that would be considered collectible art, individually packaged in attractive, compact (four-square-foot) displays, at a price the average person could afford.

The company we formed was called Gemini Enterprises. Our first factory was 400 square feet on the 6th floor of the Cable Building on Broadway at Houston Street. No air conditioning, bathroom down the hall. I loved it.

We started with six original images from artists who responded to our ads on bulletin boards at local art schools. Undaunted by the fact that neither of us had ever been in the printing business, we learned about equipment, inks, and printing processes. Before we could begin printing, silk screens had to be made. In a stroke of luck we found Alexander Heinrichi, a screen maker, just a few blocks away. One day while at Alex's to pick up our screens, I saw him pulling a proof of Andy Warhol's *Mao*. Right on the floor of the studio! I got a charge out of that. If Alex was good enough for Warhol, he was good enough for Gemini—and then some.

It was slow going at first. My partner and I were producing 100 posters a day while learning printing processes together. We both knew we needed to become better and faster quicker. To accomplish this we purchased our first semi-automatic silk screen press with drying racks. In a short time we did become good at running the equipment and increased production to about 600 posters per day with a lot less effort.

Now the ball is rolling. Posters are looking good and for the moment production issues are solved. Next up is selling the posters. We each alternated one week running the factory and one week on the road selling, driving all of New York and parts of Connecticut, New Jersey and Pennsylvania, stopping at every stationary, gift, record store and head shop that we could find. We changed the game because we supplied the stores with displays that helped sell the posters and thereby created reorders for us.

Among the first to incorporate this method, we supplied rolled posters in plastic bags with the number of each poster printed on the bag and placed into a free standing display box with a header card that had images of the six posters and their corresponding numbers. As we suspected, this bit of marketing enabled us to get our posters placed and the stores to move the goods. Simply put: "Display Sells." Storekeepers who didn't know the difference between Jim Morrison and Jimmy Carter became poster-selling geniuses overnight. Additionally, by packaging 72 or 108 posters in a display we created a bigger dollar sale than our competitors. Sales were decent but not earth-shaking. I found myself working six to seven days a week from dawn until after dark, but I was happy.

The next step was trade shows and hiring sales reps, which made all the difference. Sales began growing and we found ourselves needing more space, more equipment and more designs. Over the next eighteen months, we moved to a 5,000-square-foot loft in Soho, outgrew it, and added another 15,000 feet while expanding our line of posters. Within two-and-a-half years we had 30,000 square feet on 16th Street and one floor of a Brownstone on 57th Street and 5th Avenue, surrounded by prime retailers like Tiffany's and Saks. We also upgraded our display system to better exhibit the product by building free-standing wooden racks with pivoting wings on top, which held a dozen each of twenty-four posters.

Now we had what the big chain stores wanted and began to sell multiple units to places like Spencer Gifts and Woolco. While this was going on we ran into some trouble with Coca-Cola, the Beatles and Life Magazine over copyrighted images and trademarks. Copyright law at the time wasn't exactly crystal clear, and as we stumbled along we stepped on a few feet. If you're interested, you can look up Coca-Cola Co. v. Gemini Rising, Inc., 346F. Supp.1183 (E.D.N.Y. 1972). Some of it is pretty funny. The end result was that we ceased and desisted what they wanted us to cease and desist. We never paid any penalties or suffered in any way, other than paying a lawyer. It was kind of a kick going up against Coca-Cola. We got a lot of attention for our efforts and enjoyed every minute of it.

In the meantime, posters became a mainstream item and we grew our sales to about 2,000,000 posters a year by the end of 1972. Pretty good for a company started with $6,000 by two men who never put ink on paper before. However, all was not well.

In 1970, my partner and I had sold a piece of Gemini to a man who had been a salesman for Playtex. Steve was our sales manager, and for a while he did a great job. But as time went by, it became impossible for the three of us to get along. My brother-in-law and I agreed to sell our share in Gemini to him. I could have remained partners with Steve, but by now I felt that he would destroy the company and I would end up with nothing. I took the money, which was substantial, and signed an agreement to work for a year for the new entity to help in the transition. The agreement also included a non-compete clause for a specified period.

It was not the most pleasant experience, but there was light at the end of the tunnel. I was about to retire at twenty-eight years old. I liked that well enough. And as we all know, time does keep on moving. I had made a lot of money, and as important as that was, I also had a sense of myself as a success, was a good businessman, and had the courage to follow my dreams. I had no regrets. I would attempt something else and succeed again.

When my last day at Gemini was over, I was ecstatic. My wife, Diane, and I, together with our daughter, Robin, began a one-year trip throughout Mexico and the U.S. in a Winnebago. But that's another adventure.

Money is nice, but no man really wants to retire at age twenty-eight. Since the end of my career with Gemini, I have produced a couple of rock-and-roll concerts, written two books. I ran a café for a few years in the Coconut Grove area of Miami, worked as a wall paper hanger and in construction. But things have a way of coming full-circle. Today I am back in the printing business and pursuing a career in photography.

Someone said to me recently, "You are certainly never lacking for something to do."

My response? "I don't ever want to be that guy."

Bigger than Life

Rick Rapaport as told by Rebecca Stimson

Rick Rapaport is definitely a Millennium Man. I did not know him well. He used to come in the bookstore where I worked in Lansing, Michigan, to visit my friend and coworker, Becky Stimson. They were fast friends. Rick impressed me as handsome and friendly and humorous. Always doing interesting things. Someone you wanted to know. Good electricity is always my barometer, and Rick Rapaport had it in abundance. The title is apt, for he was bigger than life and certainly found a place to continue beyond its boundaries. This world could not contain him. Becky gladly agreed to share her story about Rick in the form of a letter.

Dear Rick,

Your 57th birthday just passed, and I was remembering a time when we were young adults and your voracious appetite focused on chocolate chip cookies, physical exercise, and knowledge. In your twenties you turned to coffee, cigarettes, and information. The same appetite drove your determination to make a difference in the world, and we are better for it.

Your friend Ann sent me your resume circa 1982. You said, "I care about the survival of the human species. I believe our situation is precarious. But if enough people work with sufficient diligence, integrity and intelligence, I believe we can back away from the abyss of extinction over the edge of which we now peer." Twenty-nine years later we're in even more trouble. You go on to say, "My long-range goals are subject to the vagaries of fluxious* circumstance. However, possibilities include any — and perhaps many — of the following: media as a writer, editor or broadcaster; politics as a researcher, press secretary or candidate; and community activism as an organizer, lobbyist or attorney." You performed all those roles — or elements of all — but the last two and one other. How I wish you'd run for public office.

Our paths crossed in 1969. You were probably in a hallway at Eastern High School making a statement with your very presence. Taller, broader, louder, smarter than most, you commanded attention without effort.

You were a leader in athletics and academics: the center on Eastern High's football field, a champion heavyweight wrestler, and the captain of both teams. You were surprisingly fast and light on your feet for such a big guy and always a force to be reckoned with because of your strength and stamina.

You were an organizer and activist even then. When the millage failed and we had to raise money for extracurricular activities, you painted PUFS (People United for Students) on the side of your beat up white station wagon. That message lasted long after our bread drives. As a senior, you were one of the founders of our alternative newspaper and the author of one of the most controversial articles: Teacher Tenure Poses Problem. That really got the administration going, you rabble-rouser. As usual, you didn't hesitate to say what needed to be said. It was only the beginning.

Whether it was a formal or informal debate—in class or outside it—you were usually the victor. Was it your bear-like physical presence? Your clear, authoritative voice? Your command of the language? Your impressive intellectual capacity? It was all those things. And your charm, too. You honed your natural gifts as the third of four brothers, sons of brilliant parents, each family member notable in their own way. But you would establish your legacy by following a very different path.

One of the class of 1972's valedictorians, you received an award from the English department and one from the student council for leadership. Your formal education continued at the University of Michigan with a Regents Scholar award, and then you went on to Michigan State University. You studied history, political science, economics, and journalism. The foundation laid by your parents and your informal education probably had as much to do with your ultimate achievements.

By the time you were twenty-five you had lived in Ann Arbor, Arizona, New York City, and Washington, D.C. But you always came back home to Lansing to mother, brothers, and friends to reattach your Midwestern roots. You left your mark on people across the country through your witty, challenging conversation; thoughtful, provocative writing; and warm and generous nature. Although you only lived to thirty-one, you accomplished more than most people do in a lifetime. You threw yourself into activism well ahead of general awareness of or interest in human rights issues or hazardous waste. Before the Internet and e-mail, you researched and catalogued humanitarian and environmental issues like a librarian. You were a great thinker and an exceptional communicator, and you shared the fruits of those gifts with your community. Whether it was your work with Robert Green, writing position papers and speech—including one for Coretta Scott King; or the Lansing Association for Human Rights, organizing fundraisers, or planning the Mardi Gras Costume Contest, you were present 110%.

That is, until you got sick.

The headaches crept up on you. They started when you lived on 8th Street, where you established your first business: Wordsmith. We carried on our conversations about current events, and you challenged me to get involved in them over cheese omelets. I remember sitting in your office surrounded by file cabinets, newspapers, maps and books, your size-huge feet propped up on the desk next to the typewriter as you read the letter you sent to the mayor and the governor and the media asking "What is your plan of action if a truck carrying nuclear waste spills on I-496?"

The headaches moved with you to the apartment above Emil's. Nastier. Like migraines. You were working on the documentary then. You got that juicer and went through bushels of apples, carrots, and beets; but your dietary changes didn't ease the symptoms. Bottles of aspirin first and prescription medication later didn't work either. The pain came and went and you soldiered on.

After you moved to the house on Michigan Avenue and started setting up your bookstore on the ground floor, the headaches got worse. You unpacked the tons— literally—of books you collected from used bookstores and yard sales from — literally—across the country. From the second floor of the house, you recovered from the debilitating pain a little more slowly each time.

By 1983, you had seen many doctors who couldn't diagnose the problem. Although you announced to them all, "I'm an active gay man. It could be AIDS," no one knew what to do then.

Finally the doctor ordered a CAT scan, and the lesions were discovered.

It was just before Thanksgiving of 1984. I was working on a teaching certificate to go with my Master's degree and called you from the MSU Union during a study break, as I often did. Your voice, usually energetic and edgy, was slow and heavy like it was traveling through a dark, deep cloud: "I'm going to Cleveland Clinic."

You did, and they removed the lesions from your brain.

Our dear friend Deri and I barreled through the cold November night with your mother, in her station wagon, to visit you. You looked the same, but your voice was different. It was higher and it wavered, changing pitch and tone. You were unsteady on your feet. The room was bright and white and pristine, and our big bear of a guy sounded like a boy and wobbled like a toddler. You came home and lived another six months.

In 1978, we took trains—you from NYC, me from Madison—and met at The Palmer House in Chicago. At dinner in a cozy little hotel dining room, you told me you were gay. In a card you sent me soon after, you told the story of our conversation. You wrote, "She looked at me as if I had said 'Pass the mashed potatoes.'" You were relieved and so was I. We talked about your journey of personal discovery and the challenges of accepting who you were while your friends and family thought you were someone else.

After that conversation, you would go on to work in Washington, produce the documentary called "Lesbians and Gay Men: the '80s" at the local cable access channel, challenge local media and government agencies about what to do in case of a nuclear spill, set up your bookstore, and live another seven years with as much enthusiasm for and dedication to your aspirations as anyone could muster.

The lesbian or gay lifestyle may be more broadly accepted now, but it was often dangerous to be openly gay in the '70s and '80s. Your coming out was a brave gift. If anything could cause people with preconceived notions about the evils of homosexuality to re-evaluate their opinions, it was having someone like you in their lives. You were so well respected that the reality — that it is character and values and deeds that matter, not who you have sex with — would surely change people's ideas of where sexual orientation fell on the list of what's important about a person.

You had an enormous effect on us. You changed our lives. We think about you and quote you and wonder what you would be doing to affect the state of the world. Most of all, we miss you. Even in death, you are still bigger than life.

Love,
Becky

* *When asked about the legitimacy of the word "fluxious," Becky replied: "I know! Fluxious?! Leave it to Rick to use a word long, long, long after common usage. I found it in Nuttall's Standard Dictionary of the English Language 1896."*

Editor's note: Rick Rapaport is the one man in this book who didn't make it to the 21st century, but I know he would've embodied the modern spirit and embraced everything with gusto. He contacted AIDS in the early days before it was understood, before there were drugs to treat it, and before doctors knew what to do about it. Rick was a man who made an impression and changed attitudes and made a difference despite his limited time on this earth. May he rest in peace and get a big smile out of this tribute to him! With special thanks to Rebecca Stimson.

Puma Concolor

Barth Satuloff

Barth Satuloff is an interesting man. He is a successful accountant who looks and sounds like one. For years he managed finances for major prize fighters like Roberto "Manos de Piedra" Durán and Hector "Macho" Camacho. I knew Barth's wife Gail first, but when my husband and I met the two of them we all clicked. Hemingway's, a bar they built in their Vero Beach home, is a comfortable, manly place as the name implies. Added to the atmosphere are a few bottles of good liquor and several mounted heads of wild beasts, all of which Barth has bagged himself on various hunts. The dogs greet us when we arrive, three hunters and Gail's Papillon, Angel. Barth finally built a dream place in the mountains of Colorado and promptly had a heart attack his first summer at the high-altitude location. Airlifted to a hospital. Long recovery. Not sure that's going to work out. But I am happy to have the Satuloffs in Florida, close to me. He wrote and submitted (and lived) the adventure described here.

Puma Concolor — the very words strike incredible fear in the hearts and minds of hunters, hikers, and naturalists. This is the scientific name of the North American mountain lion — or cougar — well-known in the western U.S. and certain parts of southern and central Florida. But it is an adaptable creature, found in every major habitat in the Western Hemisphere from the Yukon in Canada to the southern Andes in South America.

Late in 2000, after I had killed a beautiful 5 X 5 bull elk in west central Colorado on the Nottingham Ranch near Kremmling, I made the decision to cross over from being a meat hunter to becoming a trophy hunter—seeking a Colorado mountain lion. My elk guides, Dean Billington and Steve Biggerstaff of Bull Basin Guides & Outfitters, encouraged my decision and agreed to guide my lion hunt in January 2001 over much the same mountainous terrain where I had hunted elk three months earlier.

Planning for the hunt was relatively easy: booking dates, getting a Colorado mountain lion tag/license, flight arrangements, and most important—getting the right gun for the job. Robert Ruark's book *Use Enough Gun* left a big impression on me years earlier, and I found the absolute perfect rifle for the hunt—a Marlin 1895 Guide Gun, lever action in .45-70 caliber, with regular iron sights. Iron sights were very important because I would be hunting in deep snow in January at 8000' elevation, and the last thing you want happening is your rifle scope to freeze or fog up. That never happens with iron sights. The cartridge for the rifle was a 300 grain semi-jacketed hollow point bullet packing a muzzle velocity over 1200 ft. per second and muzzle energy of almost 1500 ft. lbs. (Efficacy against live targets of different projectiles and loads is defined as energy in foot pounds multiplied by projectile cross-sectional area in square inches.) This round was used by the old Buffalo hunters and had a wide reputation of bringing down any animal on the North American continent. I bought the rifle and immediately started practicing with it at the local public shooting range until I felt comfortable with its accuracy and recoil.

I could hardly wait until January 2001, when the millennium started and so did my lion hunt. I arrived in Kremmling, Colorado, two days before the hunt began on Monday. When you hunt in the mountains in Colorado, you need several days to acclimate to the altitude and lack of oxygen. Having hunted there several times before, I knew the drill well: lots of water consumption, walk around to get used to the altitude, and no alcohol.

My guides, Dean and Steve, were just as anxious as I was to start the hunt. They picked me up at the hotel early on Monday (around 6 a.m.) on a cold day (about 5 degrees F). Their hunting truck was hauling a trailer, which had a large shed-like dog box on it containing about six Majestic Walker Treeing Coonhounds, the ultimate Colorado lion hunting dog. They all had names: Candy, Blue, Reb, and so on. All were bred to hunt and track lions in both snow (wet ground) and dry ground. They were at the top of their game — a deadly game of dog versus cat!

We "cut a track" (found lion footprints in the snow) early on, but the tracks were not fresh, and eventually tapered off through snow melt. When a lion leaves a track in fresh snow, he also leaves some scent in the track, and a Majestic Walker hound (12% bloodhound) can follow that scent until it evaporates in the air or runs off in the snow melt. We finished the day without a lion sighting.

Day two and three of the five-day hunt were also not productive, even though we kept cutting new tracks in different places on the Nottingham Ranch at altitudes around 8000 feet. Day four we decided to take a break because of the weather report, predicting a heavy snow for that night, meaning fresh snow for fresh tracks on day five. So what did we do on day four? We went ice fishing on a private Alpine lake on a different ranch at about 7000 feet altitude. I had never ice fished before, but thoroughly enjoyed the time with Dean and Steve as we sat around a hole carved out of the ice by a gas powered auger, and drank Jack Daniels with our lunch to keep warm. None of us caught any fish, but somehow that didn't seem to matter at all.

On Friday, day five started at minus-7 degrees F with a huge amount of fresh snow, which had fallen the night before as predicted. Dean was the guide and video cameraman on the hunt while Steve, a highly conditioned mountain marathoner, was the houndsman whose incredible job was to run with the pack of hounds released to track and hunt the lion at 8000' altitude for hours on end without stopping. I had never seen or met anyone in the physical condition to do that.

About 7:25 a.m., the hounds Candy, Blue, and Reb cut a fresh lion track, not far from where I had shot my elk in October on the Nottingham Ranch. Steve and the dogs were off running, the dogs baying in the still, cold mountain air. There is something ancient about their cry, harkening back to when the Roman army first used them as tracking dogs thousands of years ago. The tracks led the Steve-and-dog-team up and down one mountain and onto a second mountain, about twenty minutes away from where Dean and I sat in a 4-wheel drive all-terrain vehicle, or ATV.

Steve was in communication with us using a powerful walkie-talkie, and gave us directions as to where we could find him, the dogs, and hopefully the lion. We high-tailed it over to the location he gave us and parked the ATV on an incline in deep snow. It was about fifty yards to get to the top of the incline as Dean and I trudged through the snow together. Once at the top, we looked around and didn't see Steve or the dogs, but boy could we hear the howling and Steve's shouts to us!

Our attention was directed to a stand of Ponderosa Pines about a hundred yards away, where I first saw the lion. He was about thirty-five feet up in the tree, snarling at the dogs around the base as they jumped and tried to climb the tree after the puma. "Oh my God," I said under my breath as I first saw how large, powerful, and angry this cat was. Steve was standing near the base of the tree, calling me to come closer so I would have a better shot. I was pretty confident in my shooting ability, so initially I said "No - I'm close enough!" Steve wouldn't budge his spot or his absolute insistence on my coming closer, so I experienced an abandonment of fear to come closer to the tree, also drawn by an overpowering desire to protect the houndsman Steve — at the same time not wanting to be in harm's way.

I positioned myself to shoot the lion, not broadside as most hunters might, but rather with a frontal chest shot. I jacked a round with the lever, aimed, and shot the lion in the chest with the .45-70 bullet traveling the entire length of the body, crushing bone, tissue, and organs, and exiting the carcass at the rear. The lion, still in the tree branch thirty-five feet off the ground, started flopping around, but hung onto the tree with his claws. I ejected the spent cartridge and jacked another into the chamber and fired again — this time hitting his left front paw and going through it into his jaw bone — literally lifting him out of the tree and into the air. I reloaded while he was falling to the ground, and he bounced on the frozen ground between me and Steve, two feet away from me. Then the lion rolled down a frozen creek embankment, followed by the dogs.

Steve was right behind the group with his .357 Ruger Blackhawk pistol in hand. The lion was dead, Steve was safe, the dogs were safe and not cut up, and I was safe and feeling very protective. This was definitely a major milestone in my life — not just my "hunting life" — and I truly recognized and felt it.

Later that day, we took the lion carcass to the Colorado Dept. of Wildlife inspection station in Hot Sulfur Springs, Colorado, for them to weigh, record, and draw a blood sample from the lion for a biological survey. Their old scale had rusted shut on 150 lbs. and the animal was much larger—at least 160 lbs. if not more. It was 42" in length without the tail, 36" in height at the head, and its cranial measurement was 14-4/16", just missing Boone & Crockett Club minimum of 15" to make the record books.

Before we left the Ranch, we stopped over to visit Bill Nottingham, the owner, and Susan, his daughter and ranch manager. They expressed extreme gratitude to us for protecting their resident elk herd and mule deer population from further decimation by mountain lions. They told us they had found the remains of a 700 lb. elk, which had been killed a week earlier, dragged off and eaten by a mountain lion – most likely due to their territoriality.

Even though it's a trophy, what to do with the meat? Colorado law says that if you harvest a mountain lion you must have the meat processed for consumption. They can't make you eat it—you can donate it to a charity or give it away to friends and family. I did process the meat, and after having a few bites of prepared lion steaks, decided to give it away to my more macho friends who enjoyed it.

Every great reward has a Karmic cost that must be paid. What did I receive and what did I pay for it? You decide—I already have.

From the *Peacock Throne* to the *Turban Republic*

Reflections of an Iranian about the Islamic Revolution in Iran and its aftermath

Mokhtar Shirazi

I cannot tell you how I know Mokhtar Shirazi. Nor can I tell you where he lives or what he does for a living or his given name. He has family in Iran to protect. I can tell you that this is a remarkable man as was his father before him. They take pride in their native land, formerly called Persia, rich in cultural heritage and lore. They wanted change: for democracy to come, education and the arts to flourish, and religious tolerance to exist. But Mokhtar's father saw the writing on the wall when Khomeini and the Islamic extremists revolted against the shah, and started moving his dear ones to safety as the country erupted in chaos. Few Americans know that Iranians and Iraqis were enemies, or what is really going on in the Middle East. Every book about men should contain something of politics because they shape a country's ideals and intellectual thought, influence the development of power and strength, determine policy and liberty for all, and define what we are willing to fight and die for. Mokhtar Shirazi wrote 10,000 words, which I had to cut for this book. But I keep those 10,000 words in order to have the entire picture through his eyes, knowing it was cathartic for him to tell his story at last.

Prologue

The Islamic Revolution of 1979 changed the life of every Iranian—city dwellers, villagers, the rich, the poor, the religious and the secular. It was a huge event that impacted all of our lives. As Iranians, we describe everything—every person or event—as it was before or after the revolution. This was a huge turning point in modern Iranian history. It not only changed Iran, but also created shockwaves throughout the greater Middle East—from North Africa to the borders of India.

This is my story, an Iranian boy who was eleven years old when the upheaval of this big change came to Iran. The point of this story is to explain—as I understand them now—the events I went through during the four decades in which this story takes place. This is not the most dramatic or sad story. It is one boy's story—and now—a forty-four-year-old man's reflection of the events that took place in the period before the revolution.

I want to humbly acknowledge the fact that there were many people who lost their lives, lost family members, or became victims of the infamous prisons of the shah, the ayatollahs, and the eight-year Iran-Iraq war. What happened to me and my family is in no way comparable to the people who became victims of this tragic tale.

Timeline

- 1941-1979 Crown Prince Mohammed Reza Shah Pahlavi takes his father's place on the Peacock Throne and becomes Shah of Iran.

- 1940s   Iran is an agrarian society with a feudal economic system, a minority of merchants, and traditional trades like carpet making.

- 1960s   The   shah's   White   Revolution   to modernize Iran through land reform, industry building,   focus   on   education,   and   changing archaic laws against women.

- Early 1970s   Economy flush with petrol dollars. The country is being modernized at an extremely fast pace. The shah spends vast amounts of money on weapons to make Iran a regional power and return the country to the "Great Civilization" of the Persian dynasties. The shah's SAVAK (secret police) crush all dissent, resorting to torture, imprisonment, and death by execution.

- Late 1970s   The   bourgeois   want   more freedoms as they become more affluent and educated. Opposition from the leftists/Islamists, the poor and the uneducated masses, who resent the shah for his anti-Islamic policies, is widespread. The Ayatollah Khomeini begins to stir the people to revolt. Khomeini viewed as a savior who will restore Islam and return Iran to glory.

- Spring 1978   Events leading to the Islamic Revolution begin with an article by a secular journalist and supporter of the shah criticizing Khomeini.

- January 1979   Shah Pahlavi leaves the country; seeks and is granted asylum in the U.S.

- **1979-80 Islamic Revolution.**

  Khomeini comes to power and forms the Turban Republic.

  Bani-Sader, a reformer and an economist educated in France, is elected president. Mehdi Bazargan, a pro-democratic Iranian scholar, heads interim government.

  Islamic Student Organization (fundamental Islamists) attack and occupy the American Embassy, taking over 50 U.S. hostages; demand in exchange the return of Shah Pahlavi to stand trial.

  Bazargan resigns.

  Bani-Sader takes office and, like Bazargan, encourages Khomeini to release hostages. Street battles between Bani-Sader and Khomeini supporters ensue.

- September 1980 Iraqi forces invade Iran. Iraq employs extensive chemical weapons against Iran.

- January 1981   U.S. hostages released

- Early 1980s   The war with Iraq intensifies.

- June 1989 Khomeini dies.

- 1996-2004 Khatami government comes to power. Reform strategy begins. Hope is renewed.

- The Khatami government attempts to reestablish diplomatic relations with the U.S. The Bush administration ignores the offer.

- Mahmoud Ahmadinezhad, a conservative who served in the Revolutionary Guards, is elected as president in Iran with very low voter turnout.

- Free elections are held but the vote is stolen by the Ahmadinezhad government. The people rise up. At first this is tolerated, but then a crackdown begins to restore order.

- June 2011 The Middle East is on fire. Democracy is a movement that cannot be stopped.

My Childhood

"The good old days" — that's the way I can describe my childhood. I was the youngest of five children — I have three older sisters and one older brother, and grew up in a joyful family. My father had a good job and we were relatively well off. He had come up in the ranks, starting as a maintenance shop worker in the 1950s and becoming a plant/project manager in the 1970s. My mother is an extremely caring person. Her passion in life is her children. She gave us a tremendous amount of love and we all felt very close to her. She was a true housewife who cared for us in the most nurturing way.

We were moving to different cities in Iran due to my father changing jobs as better opportunities arose. During this time we lived in company housing near the factories. These factories were usually located far from populated areas due to the pollution they create. I was always driven in a minibus or a Land Rover (which we called "service") to the nearest town to attend school. I would gaze out the window as I rode, watching the cars, trucks, and people in the small villages and suburbs on our way to school.

As with most middle class Iranians, we were a happy family. We had money, a nice house wherever we went, and would go on vacation every spring and summer. Life was improving for everyone. People were free to wear what they wanted, eat and drink what they wanted, and relations between men and women were nobody's business but their own. There were many places to go to for entertainment—from Swiss-quality ski resorts and beaches on the Caspian Sea with girls in bikinis; to night clubs, shows, theater, and modern cinemas with the latest movies.

Of course, not everyone was happy with the way things were going. The religious folks thought of the shah's policies and attempts to modernize as abhorrent. They could not accept the personal freedoms he had given the people—especially the freedoms he had given to women. Also, there were the poor and the destitute. There was a mass migration from the villages to the cities as the country began to industrialize and many wanted to live in the city and find a good job.

The pace of progress was not fast enough and there were not enough jobs for everyone, which resulted in people having to live in shacks in shanty towns surrounding the cities. The low level jobs available not only kept them poor, but increased their resentment for the shah's regime—regardless of whether or not they were religious. These people, combined with the newly emerging middle class demanding more political freedoms, created the backbone of the movement that brought about the Iranian Revolution.

I cannot say that I understood everything that was going wrong in Iran at that time as I was too young. However, I do remember a rigid class system where the people from the village were made fun of and laughed at for not being sophisticated. It was an extremely closed society and no one dared to criticize the government in public. This extended into schools as well.

I witnessed a horrible episode when I was in 4th grade. We had a poor kid in our class whose father was a simple laborer. They had recently moved from their village to the city in search of a better job. One day our teacher was giving us the results of our midterm—he would say the grade out loud as he handed us our test papers. Well, the poor kid had failed his test. Our teacher brought him in front of the class and proceeded to beat him up. He called the boy a piece of garbage whose father was a simple laborer as he slapped the boy's face and head. Then, he forced the kid to pick up a broom and sent him outside to the yard to clean a corner of the yard, in plain view of all of us through our classroom window. The teacher wanted the boy to be humiliated. Our classmate had tears streaming down his cheeks as he swept the asphalt in the school yard. He would look at us once in a while with such a broken look in his eyes that it made us all sad.

Sometimes I wonder where he is or what he is doing now. I would not be surprised if he turned into a zealot supporter of the Turban Republic—maybe he tortures people now--who knows? I often ask myself if I would turn out the same if I were in his shoes!

The Islamic Revolution of 1979

The events leading to the Islamic Revolution started in the spring of 1978. I was ten years old and on my way to finishing 5th grade. We were living in the southeastern city of Kerman, which is located on the high Iranian plateau. My father had just completed a big project where he worked and had signed a contract to initiate a project in the city of Yazd. A furnished house was prepared for us in Yazd until we settled in and got our own place. And so, we packed up our things and drove to Yazd (about six hours away). We arrived at night to a city in chaos. We could hear sporadic shooting, the acrid smell of burning tires was in the air, and tear gas burned our eyes and throats. We asked someone on the street to tell us what was happening and were told there had been demonstrations all day, many people had been shot by the army, and we were well-advised to return home quickly as the situation was fluid.

We settled in this huge old house located in the historic neighborhood of Yazd. This is a city famous for its beautiful architecture. Also, Yazd was a very conservative town. My mom and sisters had to wear the *chador* (a garb completely covering women's bodies) when they went out. We were all in shock as we had never experienced a mass uprising. At the same time, we were excited about what a new political system would be like.

One night my family was invited to a dinner party. After a few minutes of driving, we found ourselves in a section of town where the electricity had been cut off. The streets were deserted and there was no one we could find to ask for directions. It was confusing because my dad was not familiar with Yazd, and he made a couple of turns to find his way. All of a sudden we came to a section of the street that was completely barricaded. My dad stopped the car, and that is the first time I experienced the sight of a machine gun pointed at me. The car's headlights were flooding the space in front of us where three soldiers aimed machine guns in our direction.

What we did not know was that a few hours earlier a group of revolutionaries had fought with the military in the exact spot. Both sides had lost a few people and the situation was tense. The army had instituted martial law—this we did not know. My father rolled down the window to hear someone yelling at the soldiers. It was their captain telling them to open fire. My father immediately turned on the light inside the car so the soldiers could see us kids. The H&K G3 machine guns were now resting on the hood and I could hear them being cocked. The soldiers hesitated as soon as they saw the woman and children in the car with my father. They had expressions of fear and anguish mixed with a sense of duty to do their job—which was to shoot people who had ignored the martial law. They turned towards their captain, who kept yelling from some dark corner on the sidewalk to shoot us. My father used this moment of indecision to act. He put the Peugeot 604 in reverse and roared away from the soldiers, adding some burning rubber of his own to the street! Thankfully, they did not shoot us in the back.

Things got progressively worse in the following months, and my father's project in Yazd was cancelled. We moved to our hometown of Shiraz and settled in an apartment. This was the summer of 1978, and my father decided we should take my older sister to the United States where she could study at a university and return when things had settled down. At the same time, it was a good opportunity to get away from the chaos and have a vacation, so my older sister and my parents and I all left for two-months in the UK and the United States. I still did not fully understand what was happening to our country and was simply excited about going to America, where my dad had promised to take me to Disneyland. I was raised watching American movies, and saw America as the land of dreams where a kid could have lots of fun. We had a great time on our vacation, settled my sister in her new home in California, and returned to Iran.

The situation in Iran had deteriorated while we were vacationing in the U.S. Demonstrations were happening on a daily basis and many people had been killed. The workers were on strike and the economy was at a standstill. I started 6th grade in September 1978 in Shiraz. But it was a joke—all we did was chant slogans in support of the revolution to shut down the school and join other demonstrators in the street. We were throwing stones and breaking windows of other schools so they would join us as well. This was a kid having fun, and I had no real understanding of what the shah had done—only what I heard from the others.

It is sad when you realize you were used to advance someone else's agenda when you did not know anything about what you were saying. This daily routine of pouring in the streets and joining the other demonstrators continued until one day the army troops positioned in our neighborhood had enough—they started shooting in the air and pursued us. They arrested many people. I was able to jump inside someone's house and stay there until the troops had gone. After that, they shut down our school.

The situation was getting worse by the day. There were stories of lynch mobs killing government supporters in the streets, attacks on government offices, and troops shooting at the people. Everything was closed—banks, shops, gas stations, and there was a shortage of basic items. People were hoarding food and fuel. The country was in chaos and there was no rule of law. The police were too busy controlling the opposition to enforce other laws. People could get away with anything, even murder—all they had to do was to claim the person they killed was an "anti-revolutionary" or "non-believer."

A very sad and tragic element of the Iranian Revolution was violence towards religious minorities. Religious thugs and the brainwashed ignorant masses started roaming the streets of Shiraz, looking for Baha'i families. Many innocent people were killed and their houses set on fire just because they practiced a different faith. Yes, this was freedom! Freedom to kill your neighbor without cause, justified by saying that you were a true believer and that you were upholding Islamic laws and edicts. I was beginning to feel uneasy about what was going on but still had hopes for a good future, and continued to believe the promises we were made.

When the shah finally left Iran in January of 1979 there was jubilation in the streets. The people had defeated the almighty King of Kings—Mohammad Reza Shah Pahlavi.

A few weeks following his departure, the Shiite Grand Ayatollah Khomeini returned from exile and took power—the shah's regime collapsed two weeks after that. After a brief honeymoon period, the progressive president, Bani-Sader, was named a counterrevolutionary by Khomeini and forced from office. The Khomeini crackdown followed. Anyone not agreeing with Khomeini was arrested. The *hijab* (forcing women to wear Islamic garb in public) was strictly enforced. All political parties were abolished except Khomeini's "Party of God," aka Hezbollah. In 1980 Iran was invaded by Iraq.

Before these events unfolded, an interview of the new leader was shown on TV. My father told us that this revolution had been a big mistake and that Khomeini was a ruthless dictator who would ruin the country and roll back all the advances the country had made under the shah. I must admit that I was skeptical about what he said—I thought we had defeated the shah and now we would have freedom to do anything we wanted. We had never had political freedoms in Iran, so most people—I included—did not really know what this freedom would be like. We just knew that it must be a good thing.

I started 7th grade in September of 1980 in our hometown of Shiraz. The country was basically a mess, with street battles going on between the opposition and the government, an external enemy making advances within our homeland, and the general disarray within a post-revolutionary society. Government services were disorganized at best. Where we once had educated and experienced managers before the revolution, the government had installed political cronies whose only qualification was that they were "true believers." The government had also started expropriating the properties of ex-regime supporters (businesses, organizations, houses, factories, etc.).

Our school was a big house that had just been expropriated from a "non-believer." These buildings were not designed for a couple of hundred boys who were full of energy and running around all the time—the classrooms were small and we had our shop class in the one of the storage rooms. It was a joke! The government had positioned its supporters in all the schools. They were running the school affairs and the principal was just a figurehead. These so called "believers" would force us to pray during lunch time en masse. This was sad and at the same time extremely funny! They would throw a rug in the school yard where we had to line up and pray in rows. This was a disaster for the government minders who were trying to force us to be good Muslims. All we did was horse around, make jokes and play grab-ass. The mass prayer was a fiasco and they cancelled it within a week!

One day, I was sitting in the yard during recess and saw several boys my own age entering the school gate. They all looked disheveled, as if they had just awakened from a restless night sleeping in the street. They had messy hair, wrinkled shirts, and a few were walking around with simple house slippers. They were war refugees. I think this is the moment when I began to realize our country's sad and tragic condition. The expression these boys had on their faces—I can't ever forget this. They showed a combination of fear, anger and fatigue. When I was told who they were, I felt a swell of emotion about their situation. I had a tremendous hatred towards the Iraqis.

I remember wishing I could go to the front so I could kill Iraqis; of course, this was nothing but childish fantasy on my part. My parents were very protective of me and would never allow me to volunteer. Still, I was a twelve-year-old boy with dreams of picking up a gun to fight the enemies of my country. There were a lot of my classmates who joined the Basiji forces (a paramilitary volunteer force under the direction of the Revolutionary Guards—something similar to the Hitler Youth Organization) and went to the front. Also, two of my cousins joined the army and served in the front lines.

The brainwashing in the schools and the media started immediately after Khomeini consolidated his power base. The government portrayed itself as the victim of an imperialistic plot to overthrow the Iranian Revolution, with the Iraqi invasion in full force and internal fighting with opposition groups. Strict Islamic laws were written into the new constitution—all of the shah's past efforts to modernize the society were being reversed. Oppression had returned to the Iranian society, which was nothing new for us—except under the mullahs we lost our personal freedoms too. All vestiges of the old regime to include its symbol and official insignia were being removed—the Peacock Throne was being wiped off and replaced by the monstrous insignia of the Islamic/Turban Republic. Their new official insignia looked like a black spider, which is supposed to represent an Arabic phrase from the Quran meaning a combination of "Allah" and "There is no other God but Allah."

I saw this insignia on the brand new 4WD Toyota Land Cruisers, the preferred vehicle of the Revolutionary Guards. They were the most powerful force in the country by then. They were running the war and acting as the frontline security force internally. The sight of their vehicles on the streets would bring terror to all opposing the regime. The RGs were fierce supporters of the mullah regime and held themselves up as models of piety. One of their duties was to perform checks on citizens and arrest anyone with the slightest sign of opposition to the regime. They patrolled the streets and picked up students who were distributing anti-government political flyers.

As I was walking home from school one day, I heard a big commotion a few hundred meters from me. I reached the point where the noise was coming from—it was at the middle of an alley which crossed the street I was walking on. There were several Revolutionary Guards having an argument with a girl— she could not have been more than sixteen years old. I instantly recognized her as a girl who once lived in our neighborhood— she was a leftist and her job was to distribute a newspaper belonging to her organization. She had tried to sell me one of her newspapers only a few hours before, but I had ignored her as I knew what could happen if someone reported me. Now she had been caught by these RG monsters with their green uniforms, beards and AK-47s. She had a look of terror and yet--at the same time—fierce conviction for her cause.

I can never forget her face for I knew what fate awaited her after being arrested. She would be tortured in the cruelest and most vile way to make her give up the names of her friends. They might bother with a mock trial. After that, they would sentence her to death by a firing squad. To add insult to injury, she would be raped by the RGs, as the twisted mullahs believed a girl who is a virgin goes to heaven regardless of her crime against "Islam" when she is killed by an Islamic government. Yes, they would rape her to make sure she would end up going to hell after her death, shoot her, and bury her in a grave marked only by a number in the city cemetery. The terror on her face was from knowing what was to come.

I was a jumble of mixed feelings about what was going on. On one hand, I wanted to support the government in fighting the Iraqis, and on the other hand, I hated them for turning our lives into the hell it had become. I was a confused and lonely kid, as all my siblings had left Iran. My father wanted us to be brought up in a free society where we could have opportunities to better ourselves.

We moved to Tehran in the summer of 1981. By this time the American hostages had been released, but the war with Iraq was still going strong and political instability continued. We moved into an apartment my father had purchased before the revolution. However, we were supposed to have notified the local Committee office about our new apartment and the fact that we intended to move in there. This we did not do, as we were not aware of this rule. They were trying to find team houses where the opposition militia lived, organized activities, and coordinated attacks against the government. All citizens had to have a good explanation for their place of residence and who was living there. We heard a knock on the door and saw four or five Committee paramilitaries with AK-47s enter our apartment after someone opened the door. They started questioning us about where we were from and why we had not notified them about moving. Then they proceeded to ransack the place. Finding nothing *suspicious,* they issued a stern warning about obeying the security rules, and gave us all nasty looks before they left.

Government forces had the right to enter anyone's home without a court order. They would arrest family members, beat them up in front of everyone else and turn the house into shambles. Many people were taken, never to be seen again. We would hear stories from friends and relatives with family members who had been taken away. The ones who were lucky enough to be released would describe the conditions in the prisons — conditions that are too vile and disgusting to repeat here.

A recent book documented the total number of people who were executed by Shah Pahlavi and his father during their rule from 1925 to 1979. They killed about five hundred people. The Turban Republic has killed thousands, with estimates that put the total number in the range of twenty-five thousand people executed since 1979 (half the time!). It is true that even one life lost to political causes is one too many, but the comparison is striking and bears note.

The government started a program called the Cultural Revolution by shutting down the universities to revamp the curriculum and vet the faculties. All references to western culture and Iran's history before Islam were to be de-emphasized, and all instructors deemed not a supporter of the revolution were to be fired. They did something similar in schools. We had to study Arabic and the Quran for many more hours during the week as compared to before. I recall our teacher telling us that we were corrupt pieces of garbage since we had grown up during the shah's regime and that "our glorious revolution will only be fully victorious once we had died or left the country." This was of, course, great for our self-confidence!

Life continued the same throughout 1983 into 1984. The government consolidated its power base more and more. They initiated austerity plans with all resources going to the war front. All infrastructure projects were canceled and rationing of food began. Everyone was concerned with obtaining basic necessities, enduring long lines at government supported food markets and gas stations.

In 1984 I started 9th grade. I was seventeen and reaching conscription age, when I would have to register at the draft board and prepare for military service. I was actually kind of excited, as I had heard stories from the front-line and wanted to experience war for myself. My father, however, was horrified, as he knew what destiny awaited me if I were sent to the front. By then, Iraq had started using chemical weapons on a massive scale because Saddam could not stop the World War I-style human waves of the Iranian forces. Thousands of Iranian soldiers were being bombed by Saddam's chemical weapons. Khomeini did not care, declaring the war a blessing for the revolution, *a small sapling growing by the blood of the martyrs.*

My father decided I had to leave the country before I would be required to report for military duty. He consulted with his friends, and it was arranged that I would leave Iran and go to Turkey, where my father's friends would help me get to America. I left Iran in April of 1984, and after months of being alone in different countries, was able to come to America in the fall of that year. There I joined my brother and sisters.

Reflections

I started high school two weeks after entering the United States. To say that I was in culture shock is an understatement. The school was clean and organized. Boys and girls studied at the same school. I could not believe that the school teachers and administrators did not physically punish the kids. I had grown up in a system where we were constantly beaten for any indiscretion. The kids in our classroom put their feet on the chair in front of them as they listened to the teacher—we would be severely beaten for doing something like this in Iran.

I was both very excited about my new freedoms and at the same time disgusted by how materialistic and simple-minded the kids my age were. What struck me the most was that none of the kids had any clues about political issues--and on top of that—it was considered "cool" not to be concerned with such things. I thought what fools these kids were—they didn't care what was going on in their own country. However, years of brainwashing by the Turban Republic had done a job on me. I did not understand that I have to put things in perspective, and that I should not have judged my classmates according to my standards. Nevertheless, I was a seventeen-year-old kid who did not enjoy high school in America. I rarely talked to anyone and did not have many friends. I suppose I remain this way to a certain degree. I still see myself as an outsider with a unique outlook on life—one that separates me from everyone else.

And now, it is June 2011. The Middle East is on fire and the whole region has gone up in flames. Two governments have already fallen, with a couple more teetering on collapse. Some countries have crushed the protests and others have bribed their population into compliance using oil money. It is the beginning of the end for dictatorships in the Middle East. Autocratic governments — many supported by the U.S. — will fall one by one. The people of the Middle East are sick of being ruled by tyrants. They yearn to be governed by a system of freedom, justice and human rights.

Iran's Green Movement, which rose to worldwide prominence in the disputed 2008 elections, jump-started the hopes and aspirations of the people of the Middle East. This was a nonviolent and peaceful movement to bring freedom and democracy to its society and create a secular government. After thirty years, something positive had come from Iran — from its people and *not* its government. This movement will continue until the whole region is transformed to a democratic region. It will probably take years; but it is a movement that cannot be stopped!

Conclusions

First of all, I have to say that I consider myself extremely lucky to have survived such a traumatic life. There are not too many people my age who have experienced a revolution, a war, and the loss of one's country. I believe these experiences have given me a unique perspective. I appreciate the freedoms I now enjoy as I know how easy it to lose your way of life. I grew up in Iran until I was seventeen and migrated to the United States. I deeply understand both societies and what has made them what they are, but no longer feel I am understood or fully accepted by either.

I am fortunate to have had the opportunity to live in the U.S. I went to school in this country and feel I owe America a big debt of gratitude. The people of this nation are hard working and honest for the most part. Americans have always shown a great generosity toward foreign peoples. Perhaps this is because the country was formed from multiple cultures of the poor and hungry and oppressed. However, I am concerned about the lack of awareness of political issues, the role of special interests, and the lack of compassion for those who continue to seek refuge here. In addition, my experience tells me that religious fanaticism in any form in any country is dangerous and must be guarded against as a political forum. Religious tolerance is to be encouraged. Religious dogma as a means to political power is heading for trouble!

Iran is suffering from the worst kind of a fundamentalist religious government that exists on this planet. This is a government that justifies everything by dogma. They use the words of the Quran and other mullah manifestos to shut people up. They can do this easily because most people have been conditioned to fear the "wrath of God" if they disobey. But this is not a policy that will last. The youth of Iran—and for that matter the Middle East—have risen up and do not accept religious dogma as logical answers to their questions. Social media and technology have added unprecedented access to global information. The Turban Republic will be destroyed once and for all. That day may come in a year or ten years from now.

The Middle East is moving in the right direction. True enlightenment comes through education and without violence. The new generation has the potential to break the cycle of fear and violence and death. I am only one man who has seen much, but I am not the only one. Our common bond is hope for the future and the desire to live in a place where dreams can still be realized.

I have left the country of my birthplace because of religion and hatred, only to see how powerful a role they play everywhere, including my adopted country—the United States.

My hope is that my experiences will serve as a cautionary warning, but also show an appreciation for all that America has to offer. Anger and demagoguery, misguided fervor and intolerance can be replaced with knowledge, culture, enthusiasm and ingenuity. Together we have the tools to make a better world, building upon our highest aspirations for liberty and peace.

Big Daddy of Radio

Neal L. Stannard

A stage actor since 1977, Neal Stannard has appeared this year for the Vero Beach Theatre Guild in Fiddler on the Roof, Annie, Leading Ladies, *and* The Good Doctor, *and voiced the radio announcer for Pineapple Playhouse's* Steel Magnolias. *He is a news anchor and program producer for Treasure and Space Coast Radio (NewsRadio 1490 WTTB, 93.7 The Breeze, 97.1 Ocean, 99.7 Jack) in Vero Beach, and a frequent speaker at Unitarian Universalist Fellowships in Florida. He has just published his first book,* Now And Then The Movies Get It Right, *available at Amazon.com or through www.bearmanormedia.com. He also wrote this intro and the light-hearted, clever piece that follows.*

If the twin demons of Chronic Hypertension and Galloping Gouty Arthritis fail to kill me or cripple me before next February, I will have achieved forty years as a small-market radio broadcaster. (Aside from those two conditions, I'm the healthiest fifty-four-year-old male you know - which is a little like saying "Outside of that, Mrs. Lincoln, how'd you like the play?")

Although there have been detours - I'm a published author, sometime actor (many stage plays, one memorable film in which I played the assistant rapist), and have done some local television - it is radio that has put the beer in my stein and the food in the cats' dishes since '72. And it's the same as it always was in one respect: I never dread going into work. Whatever else this profession has given me, it has produced no ulcers or psychological traumas.

That said, radio in Vero Beach, Florida and neighboring cities was a vastly different animal in 1972, in two very important ways:

1) Most stations were what we called "full service," meaning you did it all: You played the records. You read the news. You read the weather. You read the sports. You read the *obituaries*. There was no CNN, no Weather Channel, no ESPN. People tuned in to be both entertained and informed, and you did it all, in turns.

2) When I say "you played the records," that meant you played *the records you chose*. For about my first eight years in the biz, there were no playlists. Your particular show might fall under a broad banner, usually adult standards (one word definition: Sinatra), rock, country, classical - under which you chose and mixed the songs yourself. You weren't limited to

the "hits." Cover versions (an artist performing a song popularized by someone else) were perfectly acceptable.

I usually worked in the adult standards format, and I had my own rotation: instrumental, vocal, instrumental, vocal. Within the instrumentals, full orchestras, from Glenn Miller to Jackie Gleason to Percy Faith, would alternate with solo instruments - trumpeters like Harry James and Doc Severinsen, pianists such as Ferrante and Teicher and Horst Jankowski, clarinetists including Benny Goodman and Pete Fountain. Within the vocals, I'd rotate male-female-male-group, because there were so many more males - Old Blue Eyes, Nat "King" Cole, Steve Lawrence, Robert Goulet.

Besides alternating the types of recording, you alternated the tempos, mixing them in a way that made sense to your ear and your soul. It was instinctive, an art form, nothing mechanical about it. No two announcers' shows sounded alike, and most had their individual partisans.

I said earlier that, even today, I never dread going into work. However, in those first years it barely resembled work at all. I'd have done it for nothing, which is just as well, because at that pay scale, I just about did.

And that's one reason why the anniversary I'm lurching towards like a herd of turtles is a unique one: because most of my contemporaries got out of the business when they realized it was never going to enrich them beyond the dreams of avarice - or even provide a bare sustenance existence. Disc jockeys learned that having fun was much more satisfying to the soul than to the pocketbook. Either they exited the profession, or they moved to its more lucrative branches: sales, engineering, or management. Those who succeed as announcers did so by moving up to medium, and then major markets - a cutthroat environment in which landing on one's rear end was just as near as the next precipitate drop in ratings.

In my own checkered career, I've set a record that probably belongs in the Guinness book: I've been fired by the same radio station (sometimes due to internal politics, sometimes due to my own shortcomings) four separate times - under four separate ownerships - *each of which eventually employed me again.* That station is part of the company I work for now, so who knows...?

In my four decades, the industry has changed in fundamental ways:

1) Except in special circumstances, the idea of a "disc jockey" choosing his own playlist is long dead and buried: prevailing wisdom says that audiences tuning into a particular station should hear the same mix of music 24/7, regardless of whatever individual announcer may be hosting the show. In

my particular company, certain stations do have selected "specialty" shows, but these are the exception, not the rule.

2) Up until the mid-1990's the Federal Communications Commission required stations to have a licensed operator on duty, signed onto the program and transmitter logs at any time the station was on the air - regardless of whether he or she was doing a live "show," or monitoring automated or network programming, a warm (and licensed) body had to be present. Because the talented and competent broadcasters did not want to work "crappy" hours, anybody willing to work weekends and overnights, and diligent enough to show up regularly, could probably break into the business - and find plenty of room to develop their skills. This came to an end when the FCC decided that broadcast automation had developed to the point that *unattended operation* was permissible. In one fell swoop, the entrance bar was raised incredibly high.

Time to pause to give credit where it's due: everyone who achieves any degree of success in his field has a number of mentors. In my case, these included, but weren't limited to, Pat Hazel, Richard Jackson, and Stanley Wood, who let an eager beaver kid hang around the station no matter how annoying he could be; Rex Rovang, who showed me how to let my imagination run wild; and Dick Crago, who taught me to temper it with mature judgment.

In later years, hanging on to lucrative employment in the field has meant adapting to a "jack of all trades" role: I write and anchor twelve short newscasts each day, and produce a number of different shows on each of the five stations in our particular company. While there are some stand-alone stations (such as the local public broadcasting outlet at the nearby state college), most are part of an umbrella operation: the more stations that can be operated by one sales-management-engineering and announcing staff, the greater the financial efficiency. (I could say "profit margin," but in this economy, that's a dubious prospect at best!)

Yeah, it's a job - a job I enjoy, but still a job. Still, in all lives there are moments. For those of us in my present company, Treasure and Space Coast Radio, those moments came during and after the twin catastrophic hurricanes of September 2004, Frances and Jeanne. Under emergency conditions, we simulcast one signal on the various stations, not only during the storms themselves but during the immediate week that followed each.

The very few of us on the air - General Manager James K. Davis, myself, and the retired "Morning Mayor of New York City," Herb Oscar Anderson, during the storms joined by Hamp Elliot, Juan O'Reilly, and others post-storm - became known as the "hunker-down heroes." I don't know that we did anything particularly heroic, but what we did do was reassure people that, like a kidney stone, "this too shall pass." (As

Davis put it, for once we were actually fulfilling our mandate of performing a public service!) To this day, people still stop us to say thanks for what we did on the air at this time, sharing information and encouragement.

For entire decades before these storms, I had worked hundreds and hundreds of air shifts in which it felt as though few, if any, were listening - and I'd better do the job for my own satisfaction, because there was little more meaning to it. Well, there was a meaning to it that I certainly couldn't see at the time. During the hunker-down period, when I found myself on the air for ten hours, twelve hours, more - every time I felt I was out of things to say, things to do, things to share, I was able to reach down into the well of experience and pull out something else.

I thank God for that unique, incredible, invaluable opportunity - at the same time I hope and pray that He doesn't ask me to do it again. But what did Jesus say? "Not my will, but Thine, be done?" I'm no one's idea of a mainstream Christian - in fact, I'm a Pulpit Supply speaker for the Unitarian Universalist Association, where we eschew creeds, infallible texts and intolerance - but in this case, the Man from Nazareth hit the bull's-eye on the nose.

Whatever minor celebrity I may have achieved, I'm still subject to the Five Stages of Fame, as is every celebrity from Rock Hudson to Rihanna:

Stage 1. Who is Neal Stannard?

Stage 2. Get me Neal Stannard.

Stage 3. Get me a Neal Stannard type.

Stage 4. Get me a younger Neal Stannard.

Stage 5. Who is Neal Stannard?

Editor's note: I first saw Neal Stannard as the man behind the scenes at the radio station when I talked about my books on air with Marcia Littlejohn. Then I saw him play Big Daddy in a summer stock production of The Glass Mendacity, *a riotous farce combining the elements of Tennessee Williams plays* A Glass Menagerie, Cat on a Hot Tin Roof, *and* A Streetcar Named Desire *(Stellaaaa!). When I did a radio interview for* The Diamond Project, *Neal signed a copy of his film book, and I finally put it together and realized that was Big Daddy at the microphone.*

This Stage of Life

Brian Stead

Something happens to boys around the age of twelve. They often have an encounter, an experience, a kind of awakening based in a mixture of hormones and awareness and discovery that gives them a sense of meaning, a sense of excitement, a sense of purpose. For Brian James Stead, it was music, and it was intensified while mastering his first guitar. My firstborn of two sons, Brian inherited my perception, independence, and wild hair (the lighter tone and blue eyes are all his own). He is curious about what lies beyond this life, beyond the confines of Earth, and who awaits him there, a recurring theme in his lyrics. Then again, he also writes party tunes like "Last Call for Monkeys" and "More Wine Than Water." He is an accomplished musician and song writer, and has a strong, clear, unmistakable voice. It would have been easy to stay home and play gigs at college bars while building a local following, but he chose to chance everything and cast his lot with the music scene in Los Angeles. In keeping with his other talents, Brian is a creative writer, too, so he found the time to tell the story of how he got from there to here. And where it will take him next.

"More songs! Keep playing! You guys rock!!" I'm outside, electric guitar in hand, the crowd around my band roaring for more. We are at a pool party in Haslett, Michigan, and this is my first real gig. I am twelve years old.

It all began with my best friend and next door neighbor, Jim Aikman. We shared a love for rock and roll, and one summer we decided to take it to the next level and start our own band. Jimmy went out and bought a drum kit, and a couple days later, I had my very first Ibanez electric guitar and a small Peavey practice amp. We knew nothing about playing these instruments, but that didn't stop us from blasting out sounds all day from his basement. We even managed to write an acceptable collection of songs and recorded a demo cassette tape under the name "Diatribe."

Something about the guitar instantly sucked me in like a tornado. It completely overtook my life and, before I knew what happened, I was devoting every ounce of my energy and time to learn everything I could about the guitar. On top of weekly lessons, my friends and I would stay up literally all night learning songs by Metallica and Nirvana, perfecting different tricks like bends and pinch harmonics.

One friend in particular, Ryan Colthorp, would soon become my inseparable pal. He was tall, goofy, and a monster on the bass guitar. He taught me a lot about music, and we began to work together, writing songs and constantly practicing. At school, at home, we always had our guitars and we weren't shy about showing off for people. Little did I know, one day we would hop in a van together and drive to California to pursue our dream.

Throughout high school, Ryan and I played in a myriad of bands. The styles ranged from funk to alternative rock, and names included Diluted, Tainted Angels, Anthem (all of these with Jim on drums), *Brokin* Rooster, and Smug, the band that would change my life forever.

I met Matteo Eyia *(ī-ee-ah)* in tenth grade and was quickly drawn to his wild and wacky personality. He was somewhat of a class clown, and could really grab your attention, whether you liked it or not. On top of that, he was a hell of a drummer, and by 2004—my senior year—Smug had formed. The lineup was me on guitar, Ryan slapping bass, and Matteo behind the drums. Even at the genesis of this band, we had a pretty clear idea of what we wanted to do with our lives...more or less, rock.

After graduating high school, the three of us moved to Kalamazoo to attend Western Michigan University, where we continued to hone our skills as a group. We rented a practice room in a huge, dilapidated, filthy warehouse downtown. Rumor had it the place used to be an institute for the mentally ill. About a dozen other hard-rock bands also played there. It was perfect for us.

We wrote a decent amount of material and got pretty tight as a live act, but when the spring semester was done, we decided to bring it back home to East Lansing. I had really enjoyed my year at college (maybe a little too much), but I felt the desire to see how far this band could take it. We had tried working with a few different vocalists at Western but none of them stuck, so it was decided I would take on the vocal duties.

I had voice lessons when younger and had experience singing in an award-winning school choir and previous bands, but I felt a little more pressure with Smug to really shine as a vocalist. We had set high goals for ourselves, and being the front man in the band came with responsibility. I was up for it though, and soon we had a house of our own in East Lansing, where we could play whenever we wanted and work on our demo.

A little over a year had passed, full of long practice sessions, day jobs, and memorable nights with friends, but we felt the time had finally come to really push ourselves to the limit. We purchased a big old beat-up van we dubbed *Bessie Blue* or *Bess* for short, made arrangements to rent a trailer, and booked one final show in Michigan to say goodbye to our fans.

I squinted through a fiery glow of colored lights to see a packed house of well-wishers. Smug was on stage at the Temple Club in Lansing, and an impressive crowd had gathered to see us perform. I was trying to wrap my head around the fact that we'd be leaving this all behind in a couple days, risking loss of the supportive embrace of our friends, our families, our *fans*. But there was a restlessness in me I had come to recognize, and I knew on some level it was time.

Our farewell show was a real mix of emotions. We kept the energy high on stage and blazed through all the songs in our catalog, throwing in a few of our staple covers, including "Purple Haze" and "Black Betty." As soon as we climbed off the stage, it hit me how much I was going to miss home. Our farewell show wasn't us quitting, it was us saying goodbye to Michigan. Soon, the three of us would be on our way to California.

"Let's go… We've got everything in here. Hit it!"

That was all it took. We were on the road. It was only a few minutes before I started thinking. *Am I really leaving? Am I really going to California?* I was!

The decision wasn't easy; in fact, it took several months of a somewhat schizophrenic hesitancy in me that ultimately came down to a last-minute decision. Even though we had been talking about it for years, I had to muster up a lot of courage to finally say "Yes, I will move to L.A. with you crazy fools!" A momentous decision after months of ups and downs, soul searching, and feeling out what was best for me. I tend to get in a rut, cruise along with whatever I'm doing, and wait for something to come along. The move to California required both decision and action on my part. I knew this was something I would regret for the rest of my life if I didn't ride it out. And, as fate would have it, one of life's major decisions was made easier because it included my two best friends. I was not alone in this.

"We're leaving in two weeks, Brian. Are you coming?"

Crunch time, and suddenly, decision made.

Here comes life at 75 mph, let's go!

It was tough, and almost hurt at first. But once I was on the road, it was the most liberated I've ever felt, and I knew it was right for me. I'd never been much further west than Chicago, let alone the West Coast! We took shifts driving and it took about five days to reach California. We slept in the van. There were so many new adventures, emotions, and so much excitement that I almost forgot we were actually doing it: driving to Los Angeles to try and make it in the music scene!

The drive took us across the country and prepared us for what was to come. After a couple flat tires (repaired by some nice guys at a garage in one of the prairie states in exchange for beer), a busted oil tank (the van came cheap but kept breaking down), and a much needed rest at a resort in Phoenix (courtesy of Matteo's godmother), we pulled our road-torn van into the bright lights of Hollywood, Calif. And we didn't know a soul. We were just happy to have clean hotel beds to sleep in and to be at our destination.

Our first week was a whirlwind of culture shock, merriment, and long hours of apartment searching. After a few days we found a one-bedroom apartment that was small (about the size of the living room in our house back in Michigan), but affordable between the three of us. It was quaint, right in the heart of Hollywood, and we had a feeling we could make it work. The building turned out to be perfect.

As we settled in, we became acquainted with the neighbors, who were mostly musicians and actors. And there was one in particular, Giuseppe, a gourmet chef from Italy who loved to cook for everyone, and became a friend. They helped us settle into the California lifestyle and really made us feel welcome and at home. I've always said that if we hadn't moved in to Yucca Street, I may not have lasted long in the City of Angels. It saved me from the revolving-door syndrome of dreamers who come to L.A. to make it in the entertainment industry and last a week, a month, three months before they give up. The support system of two close friends and great neighbors made all the difference.

With Matteo and Ryan studying their instruments at the Musician's Institute, I found a restaurant job at El Capitan, a Disney property right off the starred Walk of Fame, to make rent every month. It was surreal, at first, to be walking down Hollywood Boulevard—and just *being there*. We had arrived, I lived here now, and it was time to get to work.

As of this writing, I have lived in California for almost five years. I could fill an entire book with all the crazy experiences and knowledge I've gained about myself and the world from living in Los Angeles. It's been a lot of ups and downs, as life is, but overall an amazing journey. The greatest thing I've learned is that breaking out of your comfort zone and doing something that seems illogical and a wee bit insane can be profoundly rewarding. Stepping outside everything I knew into something I knew little about invigorated me. I took a risk, along with my best friends Ryan and Matteo, and in doing so discovered the beauty and wondrous potential of life!

Between 2006 and 2008, Smug was in overdrive mode. We played shows all over Los Angeles, including the Viper Room and Knitting Factory, and even found regular paying gigs every week down in San Diego. Ultimately, things didn't work out with Smug in L.A., but we still had a great run. I am so proud of what we accomplished. We met loads of amazing people and saw beautiful sights I never would have experienced had I stayed in Michigan. Just like back in middle school jamming with Jim and Ryan, I was still learning new things about music whether it was writing, recording, or performing. We were living a *skyless dream* (which became the title of one of our songs), and we loved every second of it.

Ryan moved to Germany in 2008 and remains a great friend of mine. Matteo continues to live in Los Angeles, and we are both still playing in (different) bands and following the love for music that drove us out here in the first place. I rented a 1930s retro-style apartment near Hollywood Boulevard with one bedroom and a great kitchen, which I couldn't fully appreciate until I had spent two years in cramped quarters with my band mates. After Smug, I took a year to focus on writing solo material and bought some recording equipment to convert my bedroom into a mini- studio. It was an interesting experience, and different from being in a band because I was the only one to make decisions and compose the music.

Recently I auditioned with an indie piano pop group called End of Ever (EoE), and in so doing found a place with the band I was looking for. They have an amazing female vocalist and three other talented, cut-up musicians. They are creative, edgy, and productive. We've made a music video and are on our way to our first full-length album. Among other bookings, we've played the Roxy on Sunset Strip, where Neil Young was the opening act in 1973. Springsteen played there, as did Frank Zappa, Bob Marley, Van Morrison, and Pearl Jam. Red Hot Chili Peppers performed their first gig with a new drummer there in 1989. I felt in good company.

Life is a circle. I'm in it for the long haul. For me, that circle is music. Creativity, love, passion, goodness, and a little craziness are included.

Shakespeare said all the world is a stage and we are all merely players. So I get up on that stage and play.

Reel to Real: On Fishing

Sean Stead

Sean Robert Stead is my son and I'm more proud of him than I can say. He has the gifts of intelligence and compassion, the ability to adapt, the desire to travel, and the willingness to succeed. I remarried and moved to Florida when Sean was twelve. He came with us for a spell, but he was happier in Michigan; and after a trial period he returned home to live with his dad and older brother. We all survived. We remained close. Thank goodness for the Internet and Facebook and phones and note cards – and jet planes. Through it all, whether it was Mullet Lake in Cheboygan, a pond in Meridian Township, the reef off the coast of Fort Lauderdale or the Intracoastal waters of Florida, Sean has loved to fish. My husband, Richard, has served as a mentor, and I have watched both of them grow in patience, knowledge, sportsmanship and awe over the years, due to the natural wonders of this pursuit. Reel to real: presenting Sean's take on fishing.

A young boy steps to the edge of a lake. In his tiny hands he holds a miniature fishing pole equipped with a bobber and hook. His father reaches into the small container of leaf worms and attaches one to the end of the boy's hook. The child sees the worm squirming and feels a sense of anguish for the struggling animal. A cast is made, perhaps ten feet from the shoreline. For all he knows, this could be where the giants lie....

Suddenly, a tug shatters the monotony that had set in for a solid fifteen minutes, an adequate amount of time to leave the boy wondering what he was doing out here. The fishing pole bends slightly and dances around, seemingly with a life of its own. The boy, wide-eyed and mouth agape, reels as hard as his scrawny muscles will allow. The battle, like the cast, is a short one. A final upward flourish from the boy sees a fish shimmering six feet in the air, arcing high over his head onto the sandy beach behind him. His father laughs, jostles his hair and congratulates him on his first catch: a four-inch bluegill. As his father holds the fish in front of him, the young boy grins from ear to ear with a palpable happiness and sense of awe. He takes a new leaf worm from the container and attaches it. The worm is hooked, as is the young boy.

The boy, now a teenager of fifteen, stands at the bow of a 27-foot fishing boat with a sturdier Star rod and a smooth Okuma reel. He skillfully baits his hook with a shrimp and casts out. He now knows the value of patience and has honed many new skills from past fishing excursions. There is visible confidence as he performs his conditioned motions with rod and reel. This patience has taught him that sometimes you have to endure significant spans of time before bagging the big one. Timing, skill and a little bit of luck determine his success. On this day he seems to have all except the luck.

His fishing partner, whom he calls Ur, stands there bringing in fish after fish. Each catch increasingly frustrates the teenager, who has caught maybe two fish, neither of which is worth mentioning. Knowing his mentor is older and more seasoned doesn't help. He sends his last cast out with the hopeful optimism that only the final shrimp can bring. Every move is calculated — it's now or never.

A tug on the line sees him tense with excitement. One big fish can erase all previous failure! He soon deflates in angst as it was just a tease, and a likely older and wiser fish has taken the final bait of the night. The boat ride back to the marina is a quiet one. The teenager is silently fuming inside, and he imagines bringing fish home to filet, none of which are his.

There is something to be said about maintaining hope; it helps keep dreams possible. But this day speaks even more about learning to deal with failure. It is ever-present throughout life, and the only mistake is allowing it to deter future endeavors, or even ruin your night. There is always tomorrow, a new chance, and a new fishing hole.

The following day he is again out on the water, this time accompanied by his mother and brother in addition to Ur. He is somewhat skeptical from yesterday's struggles, but there is magic in the air today. After a mediocre half hour, the wave begins: the older brother hooks onto a 22-inch black drum. As he brings it in, the mother's rod bends in half with a massive black drum of her own. As Ur expertly tends to their lines and they all marvel at the amazing catches, the teenager stands silently at the stern, though not in frustration. His silence is an unspoken excitement for fear of breaking the spell. One cast after another and with each a new fish is brought in. Black drum, sheepshead, mangrove snapper. It is a cornucopia of fish. When all is said and done, they return home with a double-digit haul from under two hours of angling. Sunday dinner is going to be amazing.

New chances can come when they're least expected. Sometimes the stars align to favor those bold enough to continue to try. On one particular morning, this notion manifests itself. The teenager stands on the back of Ur's boat once again as they fish together. A vicious tug on his pole is out of the ordinary and signifies a fish that he has never encountered before. The fish lays low and battles with an unorthodox pattern of resistance. There have been a slew of hurricanes that have battered Florida and the surrounding area. As a result, the waters are much colder and have brought in a few new species to the area. The fight is intense, and as the angler looks on with muscles burning, the mystery is solved as an ugly oval-shaped brown fish with black spots emerges. It lies on its side with two eyes showing. The other side is a pale white and has no eyes. What is it? "My God!" his companion shouts, "That's the biggest bloody flounder I've ever seen!" Flounders are seemingly unheard of in Vero Beach, Florida, let alone one of 24 inches. Some people at the marina still know the kid as the flounder boy.

The aforementioned Sunday fish dinner is a spectacle that he has come to know and love. The food is incredible. It doesn't get any fresher than straight from the water to the dish. But it goes beyond that. The feeling of going out on the hunt and providing for your family is an age-old satisfaction that cannot be described. The fish fries resulting from the previous excursions mentioned are ones that particularly stick out in the teenager's mind, for the adventure and experience of catching the fish adds that much more to the meal.

The teenager, now a young man of twenty-two, chuckles as he stands fishing between Ur and his brother at the bow of the boat. It is the day after Christmas and not the white wonderland he has come to associate with the holiday after years of living in Michigan. As such, this experience is somewhat surreal. He picks a spot thirty yards off between a pier and a dinghy and casts his line. A small circle in the water followed immediately by a "SPLOOSH" signifies a direct hit. He smiles and realizes the importance of taking pleasure from the little things in life, no matter how trivial they may seem.

The fish aren't exactly jumping on the hook today, but the young man looks around him. The warm breeze brings the palm fronds on shore to life, the sun casts a brilliant shimmer across the water, and the wildlife around him makes him feel a part of a true circle of life in nature. Joy is not necessarily taken from the wins and losses in life but in appreciating your surroundings and the beauty of the moment you're in.

This idea is tested as he finds himself on the losing end of the unspoken tally competition amongst the trio. Competitiveness can be an excellent characteristic to achieve success with, but if it becomes too prevalent it can strike an imbalance. He senses the moody adolescent inside him wanting to rear its ugly head and display its distaste for losing. However, wisdom comes with time and the sense to know not to let competition overshadow an otherwise awe-inspiring moment in time. Determined not to let a so-far abysmal performance ruin the trip, he thinks to himself, *I know what we're missing.* He walks to the main deck of the boat. The other two, perhaps sensing the anguished teenager in him, continue fishing without question and in silence — until the pulsing beat of the Bee Gees' "Night Fever" permeates the stale air.

The young man jives his way back to the fishing zone and casts with a grin. The bait hasn't been in the water for five seconds before he has a strike. *Stayin' alive!* He reels in and after a short battle, brings it up. The catch, a foot-long grunt, is not a take-home prize. It is, however, quite large for its species and, more importantly, quite the spectacle as it shakes and wriggles, seemingly grooving to the new tunes. The men all laugh and they continue their day with renewed vigor. Positivity is a force stronger than negativity and, when given the opportunity, it will leap to eclipse its dreary counterpart. The secret is in allowing it the possibility to transcend whatever obstacles seemingly exist.

Fishing, like life, is a series of ups and downs, successes and failures, empty hooks and record-breakers. As a boy I began to notice this trend. With the youthful exuberance similar to that of a first catch, I embarked upon life's journey and learned the value of patience, preparation and timing. Skill comes with time, and growth should accompany life's progression.

As I continued to hone these qualities, I grew as a man and gained an increased sense that things do not always go your way. There are hard times in fishing that pale in comparison to the difficulties life can throw your way, but learning to deal with failure is an essential lesson (along with the realization that at any moment a new school of fish can come to change your luck!) In addition, I saw the satisfaction gained from acting as the hunter and providing for friends and family—not only food on the table but encouragement, humor, and advice.

Now, in looking back, I see how these lessons have shaped my life and will continue to do so: the patience of waiting for any action on dull waters when dealing with people and awaiting future endeavors; the preparation of making sure all equipment is up to snuff and your game plan is mapped out in school, business, music, and travel; being a dependable friend and loyal family member who is ready to do what it takes to provide; judging success not by your performance compared to others, but how you fare according to your own standards and the extent to which it enriches your life.

I have learned much simply by standing on the back of a boat and will continue to develop as a person through the lessons of the sea, as well as those of my fishing comrades. I can tell you that while I don't yet know it all, I will continue casting, taking in the beauty surrounding me and—as always—looking for the next big fish.

Is It Fundraising or Funraising?

Karl M. Steene

Karl M. Steene is a banker by trade and raising money for good causes is part of his method. He talks to people; knows all the community movers and shakers. When he asks you a question, he actually listens to your answer. When he talks about himself, he is usually highlighting someone in his life other than himself. Karl is a good neighbor and a fantastic find. He sponsors wine tasting events and chairs road rallies and makes sure everyone has a good time while giving to worthy causes. How many people do you know in this world who spend most of their waking hours in service to others and make it all seem fun? Karl M. Steene is your man; and he graciously agreed to let me tell you his story.

This is about cool cars and making a lot of money. But first, think of your favorite cause. Perhaps it's one you give to generously or would if you could, volunteer your time with, or just agree with philosophically. Maybe it's the Rotary Club, your alma mater, a nature or wildlife foundation, education, mental health, the local children's hospital, humane society or opera guild. How about something for the Oceanographic Institute? Perhaps you'd like to announce famous speakers for the Museum of Art, lead an auction, or chair a major road rally for your charity of choice. Karl M. Steene has not done *one* of them. He has done them all.

When I Google his name I find an abundance of community activities and the subsequent praise for a man who is sincerely committed to what has become a cliché: making a difference. I find one saying as both a motto and self-suggested epitaph: *Sic Transit Gloria Mundi*, which translates to "Thus passeth the glory of the world," and more roughly, "Worldly things are fleeting." Or to quote the ancient sages who only came alive for me with George Harrison in the early seventies: "All things must pass." But until they do, Karl is determined to use the generosity of the people around him to not only do some good for the less fortunate, but to build a stronger community through solid business, ethical banking, and sound development.

A 2006 article in *Vero Life* describes Karl Steene as a man who's a ham radio operator, races sailboats, collects antique cars, and is seldom seen in a pinstriped suit. But on a sunny 75-degree day in February as I approach Karl in the parking lot of the Grand Bank, having just arrived in his candy red XLR (basically a Cadillac Corvette), he is, in fact, impeccably dressed in a navy pinstriped suit with red rep tie. He looks like a banker, and in his new position as vice president and business development manager of Grand Bank & Trust of Florida, he occasionally has to be in the office and dress the part.

Most of the time, however, he is out drumming up contacts, facilitating business, fundraising for a myriad of causes, and making things happen. Describing himself as "almost invisible," Karl states that the bank doesn't see exactly what he's doing yet, but he is confident they will. "I don't use the media to accomplish things. I am out there myself in the community, connecting people, creating business, initiating growth." He believes the Leader serves all—he gets things moving; everyone else does the rest. The results will soon become clear.

Karl has agreed to share his packet of press releases with me for purposes of this book. A handsome man, he greets me with a smile, every hair in place, a well-trimmed mustache, and blue eyes that actually twinkle — I can't help but think of Santa Claus minus the weight problem. I don't intend to interview him per se, but we start talking and it turns into one — and it is fascinating. He knows everyone, from the big-name stars with vacation homes on the Treasure Coast to the movers and shakers of John's Island; business professionals and real estate tycoons, local media celebs, restaurant and shop owners and just plain folks. He happens to be my neighbor.

Karl is not gossipy in any way. Rather, he engages contacts in a sincere manner, seeks to understand their motives for giving, and is constantly looking for ways to build a better community. He strongly believes that charitable giving and business growth go hand in hand. He is frustrated by administrators with social service skills and impressive educations but no business sense. On the other hand, he is perplexed by leaders working to solve economic problems while they themselves are taking *two* and *three* pensions; *and* returning to work or running for office and receiving another paycheck, often at taxpayer or union expense. I am struck by how genuine he is. He is not a user and can spot one a mile away.

The man is not limited to Vero Beach. His ancestral home is Seneca Falls, N.Y. where his maternal ancestors owned the local newspaper. Steene's family moved to DeLand, Florida in 1961. From the age of sixteen, he learned everything he could about banking, literally from the ground up. He started with polishing floors at a local bank and eventually became a teller. Since then, Steene has received both a bachelor's and master's degree from Florida Atlantic University. He is one of about two hundred people in the country licensed as a Certified Financial Marketing

Professional (CFMP). In banking he has worked in Naples, Coral Gables, Atlanta and Cincinnati. In 1997 he moved to Vero Beach and, before taking his current position, served as Marketing Director for Royal Bank of Canada. He hasn't time-traveled exactly, but he did bury a time capsule in 2007 to celebrate the opening of the new Indian River National Bank headquarters where he held the same position. The capsule contains money, of course: a 2007 George Washington dollar coin.

As Karl explains it, his career has never been about the money, at least not for himself. It has always been about putting money to work, making more of it to do good for others, and expanding wealth to create a healthy community in which to live. But he also strongly believes that true professional fundraisers, as in any profession, should be well paid. Another thing that strikes me is what a great time he has doing all of it. Karl Steene turns fundraising into *fun*raising.

Let's talk a little more about the fun part. Karl spent $50 on his first car, a 1955 Chevrolet. Polishing those floors at the bank earned the cash to buy a 1967 TR4A Triumph. (His favorite advisor in school made a stronger impression than she otherwise might have because she drove a yellow XKE Jaguar.) I get a huge kick out of hearing that his wife Bonnie, whom he married in 1969, drove a 1966 Mustang when they met. That happened to be my first car as well—in burgundy red—and I take a quick trip down memory lane with ol' *Ruby*. When my husband and I meet the Steenes around 2003, Karl is driving a 2000 red Corvette with white rag top. In the meantime, Karl has collected and exhibited a myriad of antique and classic cars, and his affection and appreciation for these autos is visceral.

Finally, work and play come together when Karl Steene chairs the Vero Road Rally Magnifique to raise funds for the Sun-Up Center for the Developmentally Disabled. For the uninitiated, a road rally engages the participants in the lost art of the Saturday afternoon drive, with a series of assignments and checkpoints along an established route, while raising money for charitable organizations.

The route is designed so that no car, be it a Focus or a Ferrari, has a competitive edge in and of itself. To score points, each team must answer questions about visual clues, name the make and model of an antique auto at various checkpoints (manned by volunteers), and get out of the vehicle to identify certain items. The rally covers forty or fifty miles and takes around two hours to complete. Like life, Karl promises the rally will be "fun, exciting, and a little confusing."

Win or lose, all participants are promised a Finish Line Party, a feast, award presentations, a live auction, and the chance to see some really fabulous cars. Autos known to grace the scene of past rallies range from a Porsche 911 Targa (complete with driver dressed in a tux a la James Bond and sipping a Gatorade martini—no alcohol before or during the race), Maserati, Lotus, Aston Martin, Bentley and Rolls Royce, to an SUV Hybrid, Honda Element, a two-story Harley dune buggy and a first-place winning 2005 Ford Expedition. The event has been held more than once and, under Karl's tutelage, always draws well over fifty cars. At $250 per driver and $125 per additional passenger, this is a significant contribution to a worthy cause.

Whether it's a road rally, a new cultural arts center, or the Salvation Army, there is a delicate balance Karl strives to achieve in his efforts. Do you give so freely to an organization that they cannot sustain themselves without the donations, or give in a way that "teaches them to fish"? He shares a story of meeting a man on one of the bridges to the barrier island with a rope tied around his waist. The man, i.e., the Organization hands the other end to Karl, i.e., the Donor and says, "Hang on to this while I climb over." Soon the man is lowered to a point where the donor can't hold him forever and is not strong enough to tow him back up. Does he keep holding the rope, resulting in the death of both individuals, or let the man fall to the rocks below? We both agree on the answer.

He also understands that working with non-profits is similar to marketing strategy. Everyone has their own reasons for giving or not giving. He is careful not to attribute his reasons to them. We talk about meeting the right person, asking the right question, knowing the right time. He is adept at knowing the politics of giving.

A day spent with Norman Vincent Peale in 1982 affected him profoundly. Karl didn't understand "boundless energy" at the time when he discussed the concept with the man who wrote the book on positive thinking. Now he does. (Curiously, Peale developed his philosophy initially for himself, in order to help with the enormous inferiority complex he suffered as a youth.) It is the idea that all energy flows through each of us, is available to tap into, is always available, and is what makes us feel alive. In giving it to others, we receive more in return. In keeping with Karl's vision of true philanthropy, he adds that "nearly every day I see the magic of individuals working together who draw both inspiration and energy from each other—long after our own personal time, energy and other resources have been exhausted."

The impression I come away with is of complete refreshment. Imagine a consummate professional, a banker with a strong moral code, an antique and classic car collector, a community organizer who is equally comfortable in a pin-striped suit or working the beer tent for the Rotary Club, and a family man who believes that only in helping others can we build something strong within ourselves. He always has a good story and always gives credit where due, takes what he loves doing and incorporates it into his work.

To quote the Wizard of Oz, Karl Steene is what is called a "philan...philanth...do-gooder!" And he makes a wicked lime daiquiri, too.

In Search of the Perfect Life
George W. Welker III

George Welker and his wife, Catharine ("Kitty"), have been family friends for years. George has an Episcopalian, patrician way about him that is unique to the East, stressing practicality, proper manners, and an easygoing style. He's charming and has a good sense of humor. He and his wife make you feel as if they have known you forever. So it was with interest that I read of George's experiences and learned a few things about him. He places family first. He is a salesman and a technical problem solver. Two significant events changed his life: Kitty was diagnosed and survived a couple of bouts with cancer, including stage IV melanoma; the second was the realization that he was not cut out for a business life in which he had so little control over his destiny, which led to the creation of Welpak Associates and the start of a rewarding family business. Welker has been a tennis ace, a sports car racer, an antique firearms collector and an excellent marksman. (The high-frequency deafness that resulted kept him from following in the footsteps of his father, a Navy Admiral. He did, however, pass the aptitude tests with flying colors.) George is a wonderful man to know: strong, steady, sportsmanlike, and filled with solid ideals. He loves the ocean and is intrigued with space exploration. He gives credence to the maxim that the successful voyage remains steady as she goes.

My early life was exactly what one expects in a career Navy family. I was born in 1938 in the Chelsea Naval Hospital, Boston, Massachusetts; and three weeks later my world had moved west to Honolulu, Hawaii. As a toddler, I somehow contracted polio resulting in paralysis of the left side of my body. My mother took me into the warm Pacific surf every day for six months and I was back up and running by age two. I even managed to crash the stage where Hula Hattie was performing with her entourage and amused the audience by trying to imitate her gyrations. I did that more than once, but never did get the hang of that dance. My father was transferred to the Navy Department in Washington, D.C., just a matter of weeks before the attack on Pearl Harbor. Talk about good timing!

Following his involvement with the code breakers (including the German Enigma machine) in Washington, Dad was sent to the South Pacific to command one of the few warships the U.S. had to throw up against the Japanese fleet that was already there. His ship was a destroyer, also known as a "tin can" because of its light armament. It was a pretty lopsided affair in those early years of the war. I will never forget my mother gently preparing my two sisters and me for the very real possibility that we would never see our father again. What a difficult thing to have to do with three small children, but you had to know my mother. She was unusually strong and in control, even under the worst of circumstances. We lived out the remaining war years in Coronado, California. I have many positive memories of that time, despite rationing, blackouts and air raid sirens. I guess that falls in the category of not knowing any better.

After the war years, we moved frequently and Dad's assignments often took him overseas alone. Looking back, I realize that anyone born into the military learns some formative lessons that follow throughout one's lifetime. Some of those life lessons are sad in a way, particularly the ones about not letting your roots grow too deep in any one place and accepting the fact that childhood friendships are often fleeting and temporary. The good ones involve learning to be flexible and adaptive. Dad retired from the Navy with the rank of Rear Admiral at the age of fifty. We lived in a wonderful old Victorian house in Chevy Chase, Md., just outside the Washington, D.C. boundary.

We subsequently moved to a working farm in northwestern Montgomery County, Maryland, roughly twenty-five miles from Washington. I spent most of my junior high and high school years living and working on that farm. What a fantastic learning experience that was! In addition to getting up close and comfortable with the ways of nature, I learned what hard work and persistence are all about. In my junior year at the small local high school I met a remarkable young lady, Catharine Ginn, who moved to the area from Gates Mills, Ohio. I was one of the school jocks and she was a cheerleader. She and I became the absolute best of friends, not realizing at the time that we were destined to spend our lives together. I moved to a bigger down-county high school in my senior year and we subsequently parted ways for our respective universities, Penn State and the University of Miami (Florida).

Penn State was a real awakening for me at age seventeen. In addition to taking mechanical engineering and Navy ROTC, I also played freshman basketball and pledged a fraternity (Phi Gamma Delta). To call that total overload would be a major understatement! To survive scholastically, the basketball and fraternity fell by the wayside. I did manage to recover, rejoined the fraternity in my junior year, and continued my education on a more normal footing. During my senior year, several of my fraternity brothers and I decided to visit the University of Maryland, where "Kitty" (Catharine) had transferred after her one year at Miami. We made that trip several more times and Kitty and I reconnected. I graduated in 1959 with degrees in engineering and business administration, and decided to take a fling at the business side of my education by joining a large stock brokerage firm in Washington. I can't be sure, but the University of Maryland's close proximity might have had something to do with that decision.

During that time, Kitty's family moved to the Easton area on Maryland's eastern shore, and we spent many wonderful times sailing and powerboating on the Chesapeake Bay and its tributaries. We even had to pay the princely sum of $4.00 a bushel for fresh oysters purchased directly from the oyster boats plying the waters in front of the family home. Kitty and I were engaged during her senior year and married shortly after her graduation. We resided in Bethesda, Maryland, another Washington suburb, while I continued with the brokerage firm; and we traveled back and forth to Easton on weekends. It was a great way to kick off a marriage! Scott, our first child, was born in 1963 in Washington, following my active military duty in Columbia, South Carolina and El Paso, Texas.

Over time, I realized the brokerage business was not what I wanted in the way of a career. I was subsequently recruited to join the Wm. S. Merrell, Inc. corporate management development program. My first assignment (or test) was to take over an established sales territory from a seasoned veteran salesman and then boost sales substantially. That twelve-month assignment taught me a great deal about setting ambitious goals and devising ways to achieve them. I also learned that I could sell. The company moved me to their Cincinnati, Ohio headquarters, where I went through a succession of marketing, promotion and sales training positions. I was headed for field sales management until someone discovered that I also had an engineering degree that could be put to use tackling some pressing technical challenges in the manufacturing operations.

Word got around about my problem solving skills, and several large pharmaceutical companies contacted me about switching horses. Our daughter, Stacy, was born in 1965 in Cincinnati.

I accepted a position with Merck & Co., Inc. and we moved to southeastern Pennsylvania in 1967. Shortly thereafter our son, Todd, was born to complete our family. Despite the imposition of a long commute, we chose to settle in Chester County, Pa., and have never looked back. During my years with Merck, I became active in several professional associations including the AMA, Society for the Advancement of Management, and the Packaging Institute, Inc. My charge at Merck was to identify and introduce new packaging technologies to the company to reduce costs, improve product quality, and foster regulatory compliance. I guess I did it well, because I soon found myself across town at Wyeth Laboratories, Inc. starting up a new staff operation focused on packaging technology. We didn't even have to move and my commute got much shorter!

I spent the following ten years (1970-1980) pursuing and managing packaging technologies for Wyeth. Responsibilities included packaging development, specifications, graphics, printing, automation and anything else involving the technology that no one else wanted to tackle. Our division supported packaging operations in numerous North American Wyeth plants. We grew the division and enjoyed numerous successes. I was promoted to Director and put on the short list for the Vice President of Operations slot. During this period, I learned something about myself that I had not realized before. The fact of the matter was that I probably was not cut out for the confines of corporate life. I needed more freedom and fewer constraints.

In 1980 I resigned to start Welpak Associates, Inc., a full-service sales and consulting company focused on — what else — packaging technologies for the pharmaceutical industry. My two largest customers to start were Merck and Wyeth, which I guess says that I was sensible enough not to burn any bridges. Welpak grew over the ensuing years and is now in its thirty-first year of operation. Kitty and I managed to put our three children through college and enjoyed a great deal of domestic and international travel together. We also purchased the first in a succession of oceanfront condominiums in Ocean City, Md. We still enjoy long weekends in Ocean City with family members between May and October. It is safe to say that we love the sounds, sights and smells of the ocean.

Kitty and I moved twice more in Chester County, once to build a new home roughly a mile from the house we bought in 1967, and once again in 2008 to build another house in Kimberton, Pa. where we reside today. We are blessed that all three of our children and seven grandchildren live close by and we see them often for family events. I should add that both Scott and Todd joined Welpak after garnering corporate experience elsewhere. They became the driving force to expand our company beyond the pharmaceutical industry into foods, beverages, household and personal products.

As I sit here in 2011, I look back with great fondness to all of the wonderful experiences I had and all of the wonderful, talented people I had the good fortune to meet, both professionally and personally. While still active in our business, I am systematically throttling down my activity, travel, and customer responsibilities. What that really means is that I am freeing up most of my time to enjoy the love of my life, Kitty. She has been an inspiration to me in every possible way, and has supported me every step of the way through thick and thin. I am truly a lucky man. She and I will enjoy every moment that God grants us from here on.

Steel Oak

Lawson John Whiting

Lawson John Whiting is yet another fine gentleman and great all-around guy I met through my husband. This time the meeting was at their class reunion (details below). From the talk ("discussions" to men) going on around me, I gather that Lawson had his share of trouble and shenanigans in high school and that he was quite the ladies' man. Today, he is faithful (married happily to the same woman for over 40 years), polished, still handsome, and a kick to be around. There's a bit of an edge to his opinions I really enjoy. His career years were spent in the steel business, and he personifies quiet strength. How do you reconcile the steel of youth with the soft patina of advancing age? Read what I have to report about Lawson and you'll have a pretty good idea.

I first meet Lawson J. Whiting at the 50th class reunion of Malvern Prep School in Malvern, Pennsylvania. I'm attending with my husband who graduated the same year, though all alumni are invited to opening night of the three-day festivities. Richard is really looking forward to meeting up with Lawson again. I, on the other hand, am looking forward to watching a bunch of aging preppies talking about old times, golfing, eating and drinking, calling to mind experiences I have nothing to do with, and hoping to get along passably with one or two of the wives who attend. These pleasant thoughts aside, I plan to be a vision of grace and calm.

We're staying at the Desmond Conference Center and Hotel in Malvern, along with most of the attendees for this event. The place features classic colonial décor, a large, Tavern-on-the-Green-type lobby and outdoor dining area, and lots of paintings of the hunt. The Fox and Hounds Pub boasts the original mahogany bar and glass panels from an English Gentlemen's Club. A wedding party is also lodged at the hotel, which features one of the area's premiere ballrooms; and as I wait for my husband to join me in the lobby and Lawson to pick us up, I see a parade of men in tuxes and women in dresses that would only be worn to a wedding pass by me on their way to the reception.

Lawson arrives in a black luxury Toyota Avalon, and I am pleasantly surprised. Malvern graduates are proper and polite to a fault, but Lawson is genuine and clever and gallant. I will have one other person to talk with at the reunion while my husband reminisces with former classmates. After, a smaller group meets at the General Warren Inne, an historic tavern and lodge built in 1745 as a premier carriage stop for hungry travelers. It has been renovated and restored over the years, but retains its colonial character. Owned by John Penn (grandson of William Penn) during the American Revolution, it became a Tory stronghold where Loyalists met, drew maps, and plotted against the revolutionaries. In 1825, in an attempt to make amends with the new independent nation, the inn was renamed the General Warren for the American hero of Bunker Hill. In 2005, improvements included the Admiral Vernon Dining Room and the return of the Warren Tavern, a spacious, wood-beamed bar, relocated to its original spot of the old tavern from the 19th century. In a bow to the modern age, this information and more is found on their website.

Anyway, we get through the campus tour, drinks and dinner; the requisite show of pictures and past achievements at the reunion. Later, everyone who shows up at the General Warren begins to relax and unwind a little more in the cozy, wood-smoke atmosphere of the Tavern bar. Tommy's there, the bartender, whom Richard has known for years. Richard is in heaven being at a place where he's recognized and knows everyone; buying drinks, holding court. The next morning I go downstairs to breakfast alone at the Desmond while my husband gets another hour of much-needed rest and recovery. Lawson has made the trip unaccompanied by his wife Patti, whom he married in 1965. He is seated at a table a short distance away. Dressed in an oxford shirt and khakis, he calls to me and I sit with him while he finishes his coffee and I wait for my scrambled eggs and orange juice to arrive.

For purposes of this book, Lawson is my man of steel—literally the industry he was a part of for forty-seven years. I am interested in learning about the steel business and think it will be a good fit for the book. But when I interview and research the man, I come up with this family tree that goes back to John Whiting born in 1540 in Essex, England. From there I find ancestors in Boston, Lincolnshire, England; then Shirbeck, Lincolnshire; but by the end of the 17th century Oliver Whiting is in Pensfield, Monroe County, New York. I follow the line and locations: Tewksbury, Massachusetts; Pensfield, Cornwall, and Webster, all in New York; back to Penfield (the "s" is suddenly dropped and remains the proper spelling to this day) and then Pennsylvania, USA. Lawson's father is born in Brooklyn, New York, but dies in 1997 in Delray Beach, Florida. The first "Lawson" crops up in 1854 and it becomes a popular family name. At last we come to our man Lawson John Whiting born in Bayshore, Long Island, New York, followed by son Lawson Edward who is born in Pittsburgh, Pa.

With all of the recent historical tie-ins at the reunion in Pennsylvania, I feel the need to tie some of this in here. I've always been amazed by the sense of place people in the Northeast have. Because families stayed close geographically, they were able to maintain detailed ancestral records, and since the area has the distinction of being our nation's birthplace, it's all so *preserved.* And yet, the past becomes alive in the preservation.

Getting back to steel, Lawson is from the generation that had lifetime loyalty for employers who were in turn loyal to their employees. Almost unheard of today, he had every intention of spending his entire career with the same company. He worked for U.S. Steel until 1985, when he was fired at the age of forty-four because his boss... let's just say he couldn't get along with him. This was traumatic. He knew nearly everyone in the business and was generally well liked, but few if any positions were available as the steel industry began its decline in the '80s. The economy made it tough going. A national manager of sales for tin mill products (tin cans, oil cans, gas cans, and baking pans etc.), he had traveled extensively for years. With a generous settlement and some consulting on the side, Lawson decided to take some time off and get to know his kids, son Lawson and daughter Brooke.

After six months he began looking for work in earnest. But leaving a job is like removing your hand from a bucket of water. How long does it take for the water to fill in as if your hand were never there? Suddenly it was, *"Lawson who?"*

It took nine months. He wound up with American Shear Knife Company (ASKO) in Pittsburgh, as VP of Sales. The company makes slitting machines and rotary knives for cutting steel plates that range in size from 6-inch plates to 160 inches long, a foot high, and a half-foot thick. They are used in steel processing. The man became expert in the field. I don't understand it all, but Lawson does. He actually wrote the book on the subject in the chapter "Shear Knives" from the *Handbook of Metalforming Processes*. It's available on amazon.com for $200 if you're interested.

Lawson eased into retirement, moving his office home and working from there for two years prior to calling it quits. This happened fairly recently, and Lawson is still reexamining his life and deciding where he wants to go from here; what the next phase will be. Initially interested in a move to Florida to spend his Golden Years, grandchildren changed all that, especially for his wife. Daughter Brooke and her husband Jeff have four children together, the youngest of whom offers the family the challenges (and joys) of Downs syndrome. Lawson and Patti became lost in the school activities, soccer and football, doctor and dental appointments of their grandchildren.

Brooke and Jeff have purchased a dilapidated house built in the late 1800s, with tiny rooms down, three bedrooms and a bath up, a three-car detached garage, an outbuilding, and one of the few remaining octagonal-shaped barns. The barn has an upstairs apartment, another three-car garage rented for antique auto storage, assorted farm artifacts, antiques and junk. They have worked with contractors to add another 4,000 square feet of living space in the original house, connected the garage, expanded and modernized the rooms. There's a computer center, a kids' corner, a master bed and bath. Surrounded by a white fence, which is surrounded on three sides by an eleven-acre township park, they have more outdoor living space than most people in Pittsburgh could ever dream of. The house is five hundred yards from the Whiting homestead, a nice walk or a short drive away.

Recognizing that on some level Lawson has made the decision to remain in Pittsburgh, I ask him what, if anything, appeals to him about living there. He is quick to respond that he has been a member of the St. Clair Country Club for thirty years. He and Patti have many friends there. He is a golfer. I jump at the mention of the sport, always curious about the reasons for its appeal. Lawson echoes the thoughts of many of his fellows when he tells me that golf is his chance to be alone, to find camaraderie with other men, physical exercise and sunshine. He adds that he enjoys the challenge to play better. Congenital back problems resulting in five major surgeries have prevented him from pursuing this activity as much as he would like, but he enjoys it no less.

We drift into talk of his cultural background, which is English with some Scots/Irish. His father sold Hearst syndicated comic strips to small town newspapers. His son Lawson Jr. studied in Ohio, worked for a trust bank in Florida, and then transferred to Chicago where he earned his MBA. In merging and acquisitions, he landed a position with the Louisville based distributor Brown-Forman (Jack Daniels, Finlandia vodka, and many other popular brands) and is currently based in London, England as VP of Finance & Director of Strategy for Europe and Africa. He lives in Surrey with wife Debbie, who is from Louisville and longs to return, and their three children. So, in a way, the son has returned to the family base.

What forms the strong roots of a family tree and serves us even as branches spread, children flower, seasons pass? By the same token, what does history teach us? Is it just a bunch of useless facts and dates or does it have something to offer us in real time? Does history repeat itself or are we constantly evolving in new ways? To paraphrase Napoleon, "History is the past agreed upon." It is written by the victors. Conversely, it is rewritten by the forgotten as they stand up and find their voice, filling in the missing points and lost details on the timeline. When lessons of the past join with the present—when we strive to view the entire picture—the future can only be brighter.

Lawson John Whiting forged a career out of steel, provided for a family based in solid roots, and used history to find meaning in the area in which he finds himself; and as a vehicle to make life meaningful and good. When he hits that golf ball he is in the moment, the past converging, the future full of possibility. Only green velvet expanse, blue skies, and the *whoosh* of the club as it connects with the ball and sends it soaring into the wind.

Breaking Even

James Aikman

The deadline for submissions was May 25th, and I had given up on receiving something from Jim, when his e-mail popped into my mailbox. It was 6:38 p.m. on the 1st of June. It was just the one I had been waiting for to complete the book. That is why it is saved for last. James Aikman is a mountain climber and a film maker; and by some miracle of his own making, he has found a way to do both for a living. In 2008 he was hired as a right-hand man for Sender Films in Boulder, Colorado, a leading producer of climbing/mountaineering and related films. There he worked as a producer, director, editor and cinematographer, and oversaw post-production. In 2010 he switched to freelance film and photography, starting Jim Aikman Media Solutions (www.jimaikman.com) specializing in outdoor, adventure, and commercial/promotional media. A graduate of the University of Michigan, where he studied film studies and English, he has combined his education and life passions with work he loves to do. In recent years he has traveled to such diverse places as Nuevo Leon, Mexico; Alaska, Southeast Asia, Peru, Puerto Rico and Kathmandu. His photos reflect perceptive intelligence and a sense for color and light: a bowl of food, a junket in the rising sun, a mountaintop in Nepal, a strikingly handsome Jim sitting at a table surrounded by beautiful young women. I have known Jimmy since he was a boy and recognize the passion for life he possesses. The following describes both the wonder and the angst of youth, when everything is possible, eternal secrets wait unfolding, and the world begs for exploration.

I am addicted to flux. Constant change; ebb and flow; diversity of life and color and faces, places, things. I'm always reluctant to tell people about my lifestyle and dreams, lest I jinx them and resolve myself to a more routine and, yes, ordinary life. I find it difficult to talk about myself, almost ashamed of the reckless abandon with which I greet challenges, blindly charging towards this glowing idea of myself that I've cultivated for the last decade. But it becomes an illuminating process to turn the lens on myself, and I proceed with fingers crossed and one eye closed.

I've been off the road now for three days and already I am terribly depressed and yearning for the next exodus. I try to approach idle time with motivation and foresight but usually just end up feeling utterly alone and stagnant when I'm not traveling and pushing my limits in strange places. Satiation at home has been hard to come by.

When asked *why* I have this aversion to "home," I admit that it means the end of something grand and ephemeral—a call to rest and recuperate. As if I'm ready for that! While I understand the need for recovery time, I also have my best night's sleep when I'm furthest from my mailing address. This restless feeling of not having a home translates into *where I am* is home. And so, I call the journey itself my hearth, the bounty of life my pillow.

Perhaps this wanderlust is just a phase and I will eventually get it all out of my system and find peace in consistency; but sitting here now with my feet tapping and mind racing, I cannot imagine reaching that eventuality. But I am not a spoiled bohemian from Trustafaria, nor am I a destitute climbing bum scrounging my meals from dumpsters. I work hard when the opportunity is there, with maniacal devotion to my craft, and somehow manage to break even financially, which for me is the perfect equilibrium. Work hard, play hard—and somewhere in the mix try and get a few hours of sleep.

In the last three years, I have fallen into a crevasse in an Alaska glacier, been blessed by Buddhist monks in the Himalayas, watched the sun rise on Machu Picchu, spent weeks at a time off the grid without phones or computers, and climbed everywhere along the way. I've made this possible through a fusion of my passion for filmmaking and my obsession with adventure.

Since I finished college in 2008, I have worked on and off as a producer of rock climbing and adventure documentaries and feel so lucky to have landed in my dream job at the tender age of twenty-five that I often wonder how I can keep it going. I am currently building a freelance career, where all scheduling, producing, and traveling are organized and executed by me. Sometimes this lifestyle bears the most rewarding fruit I've ever tasted; and sometimes, like today, I find myself overwhelmed by the daunting task of going at it alone.

When I sit down to write these words, it feels dangerously close to an ego trip. But I'm just trying as hard as everyone else to find what makes us happy human beings. What makes that monkey on your back hop off and dance around with exalted freedom. So, rather than chronicling my experiences in any kind of autobiographical form, I have pulled a series of passages from the journals I've kept since 2009. Some are tormented, others ecstatic, several deeply personal, and all inspired by my life on the road, in the air, and on the wall.

Someday I will have to go back through all these experiences and try to make some sense of them, perhaps with a pen and paper; but only some of them bear recalling. My episodes of excess, characterized by drinking, climbing, and exploiting the world for my own titillation, are less needing of a record because their actualization was so fleeting and thus spoiled by my frivolous musing. Those moments are better experienced and left as they are. But the moments of ecstasy and despair in far corners of the world are what really need recording, lest they fade into obscurity.

There is something so empowering about feeling expert at this wandering, especially times that would make some people tear their hair out, but make me dance a jig in the soft moonlight.

This world is such a subtle monster, and it really takes more time, more suffering, and more success to feel even a tinkling of cruel understanding. Infinite possibility, desires, beliefs; railing against my fears about the world, and myself, and love.

It's too easy for me to get wholly caught up in myself and my ego and my work, and even pursuits of self-improvement or keeping busy, making every day unique. But life is not thus, no matter how hard I try.

Irresponsibly hurling myself around the world...

These moments in life when you actually feel a tactile and definable pain in your heart or soul or whatever it is are few and far-between, and never forgotten. On the contrary, I grow in leaps and bounds from those times and that hardship, though I never wish it upon myself.

Squandering my talent on reckless masturbation and cigarettes...

Why is equilibrium so hard to find? I'll die without it, or maybe it is death. Maybe it's a blessing to avalanche through life, sweeping every experience into the chaotic trail I leave behind, constantly crushing and constantly deconstructing, allowing me to rebuild.

To live life with such polarity, emotional turbulence – like a child scorned, humiliatingly proud, stubborn, confused – such complex and profound feelings serve so powerfully to ingrain these experiences and make them unique. And give me the time and resolve to move on. Not so serious… living for one's self, protecting the heart, imprisoning the sentimental despair; to be outwardly at peace. And strong.

It is so liberating to travel alone, no egos to fan or fancies to tickle. Other than my own, of course.

Hopefully enough, but not too much.

Inward. Look inward. Mindfulness. Less escape, more presence.

Everyone compassionate, everyone selfish, everyone cruel, everyone forgiving, even when in disguise…unsettling to live without an antagonist.

I make these trite attempts at sweeping humanity up with this narrow idea of circularity, equilibrium, karmic balance, the before and the after – the horrible truth that life carries on in everyone's absence. Tiptoeing this line, peering over at oblivion with a playful sneer, and contempt for any force that claims to be stronger than the mighty I.

Making a home in my search for it. The end of the rainbow doesn't really exist, the means are the end! Just keep searching and at the very least I might fill up a few more journals with foolish ideas.

Continuing to blow up my "normal" perceptions into a million tiny pieces that slowly coagulate back into a new sense of reality.

Always so much apprehension in the uncertainty of returning home, as opposed to leaving it. Comfort found only in adversity, following a challenge in a distant resting place.

Maybe redemption arrives at the end, in the epilogue.

The year 2010 was about escape, running to the extreme corners of the grid to somehow put the main stage behind me and seek the place where it could not find me; but 2011 will be (and has been) about exploring and integrating into the boundless immensity of life — without prejudice.

Floating between continents on planes large and small, old and new, jet and turbine, like the places I go, bound together by this network of airborne combustion, compounding my perception of life on this planet to an increasingly narrow scope of an expanding landscape — or broadening scope of a shrinking landscape, depending on when you ask me; my preponderances routing and evolving on a sliding scale, constant and flowing, like the tide of the Pacific Ocean seen from the tiny dwelling of an intrepid sea crab. How to reconcile these reckless spoils? How to quell this guilt from chaotic self-indulgence?

That's not how I intended it; I'm just trying to shoot the moon, go for broke, say YES to all life's glorious opportunity and somehow shrink it down to something I can fit in my back pocket and thereby come to control it, or govern it, or at least understand it to the extent that I grow as an individual citizen of this reality and find some peace with its endless imperfection...ingesting all the world's great flavors to develop a truly defined and informed palate: a taste for the world's diverse and intoxicating colors.

The End

CPSIA information can be obtained at www.ICGtesting.com
Printed in the USA
LVOW091244210911

247247LV00001B/2/P